CAR NATION

James Lorimer & Company Ltd., Publishers acknowledge the support of the Ontario Arts Council. We acknowledge the support of the Government of Canada through the Book Publishing Industry Development Program (BPIDP) for our publishing activities. We acknowledge the support of the Canada Council for the Arts for our publishing program. We acknowledge the support of the Government of Ontario through the Ontario Media Development Corporation's Ontario Book Initiative.

Library and Archives Canada Cataloguing in Publication

Anastakis, Dimitry, 1970–
        Car nation: an illustrated history of Canada's transformation behind the wheel / Dimitry Anastakis.

ISBN 978-1-55277-005-4

        1. Automobiles—Canada—History. 2. Automobile industry and trade—Canada—History. I. Title.

TL26.A53 2008   388.3'420971
C2007-907496-0

Visual on adjacent page: Sectional view of a Franklin motor (note the hand crank), from *Instructions concerning the Care and Operation of Franklin Motor Cars*, 1910

Canada Council   Conseil des Arts
for the Arts   du Canada

ONTARIO ARTS COUNCIL
CONSEIL DES ARTS DE L'ONTARIO

James Lorimer & Company Ltd., Publishers
317 Adelaide Street West, Suite #1002
Toronto, Ontario
M5V 1P9
www.lorimer.ca

Printed and bound in China

CAR NATION

An Illustrated History of Canada's Transformation Behind the Wheel

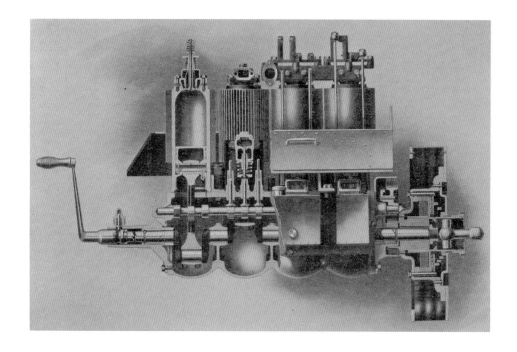

DIMITRY ANASTAKIS

James Lorimer & Company Ltd., Publishers
Toronto

For my son, Jack

Contents

Machines, People, Places and a World Transformed

There had been, before the car, other machines that changed the world. The printing press, the steam engine, the cotton gin and the telephone all have their place in history. A few of these momentous machines even have special connections to Canada. Alexander Graham Bell inaugurated a talkative, smaller world when he placed the first long-distance telephone call from Brantford to Paris, Ontario, in 1876. The railroads, of course, were not invented here, but the singularly amazing feat of building the Canadian Pacific Railroad across Canada in 1885 forever transformed the country and remade the northern half of an entire continent.

But the car was the machine that truly changed the world. From the time of its first appearance in the late nineteenth century, the automobile has had a more profound effect upon people and their environment than any other machine in history. Since then, the television, the computer and the Internet have changed how people work and communicate, but they have not shaped as many aspects of human life. In Canada, the car changed how we design our cities and homes, the way we travel and work, how we socialize and court — even the very air we breathe.

As a machine, the automobile emerged as a realization of centuries of human innovation. Old and new crafts and skills as diverse as rubber-making, wood-working, steel-forging, oil-refining and a host of other advances all came together in a perfect technological symphony. These technologies were combined in dramatic new processes that changed the way humans worked. The manufacturing of parts, engines and tires; the moving assembly line; the advertising and sale

The world before autos: Wilfrid Laurier waiting for a train, Ontario, 1904. By the end of his time in office autos were becoming a part of the Canadian landscape.

Henry Ford, 1863–1947, in his "quadricycle," built in 1896. Below: An antique car side lamp, which reflected early automobiling's wagon heritage.

of cars; and the maintenance and repair of cars ushered in new production techniques, new modes of communication and expression and entire new industries and services. The car became the exemplar of the system that had produced it, and that it had produced: the modern capitalist economy.

Machines are a technology, but technologies are socially constructed, none more so than the automobile. In its manufacture, use, sale and purchase, it became a fulcrum for human interaction. Desire, need, necessity, expression and emotion were as much a part of the automobile as were pistons, tires, headlights and the steering wheel. From the first moment people saw the car, they fell in love with it, were scared by it, mesmerized by its potential and enthralled by what it could *do*. It became the personification of freedom, an outward indicator of Canadians' aspirations and dreams.

The bond between the machine and the people was instant and unbreakable. The car became our way of life, and soon people could not imagine a world without it.

Through the car, machines were connected to people and, ultimately, to places. Cars remade the very landscape they trundled across. City, town, countryside and the places in between were changed by the arrival of the automobile. Where people were once isolated, made distant by barriers to travel and interchange, the car exploded the constraints of time and space. Now, humans measured their movements and migrations not in weeks, days or distances, but in hours.

The story of the car in Canada is both unique and similar to the many other national histories of car, people and place. In a large, sprawling and geographically difficult country such as ours, the automobile could only have an ever-changing impact. Cars were quickly adapted by Prairie grain farmers, by travellers to the north and by rough-and-tumble adventurers looking for a thrill by traversing the immense span of the country. If the railways were the sinews that bound Canada together as a nation in the nineteenth century, the automobile was the symbol of what many considered the modern Canada of the twentieth century, and the final victory of technology over landscape.

Canada's unique story was also influenced by its location: proximity to the United States was both a blessing and a curse for Canadians and their connection to the car. Abutting the world's greatest automobile society meant that Canadians were also pioneers in the early use and production of cars. America's embrace of mass automobility spilled over into Canada: the democratic impulse unleashed by the car quickly

A 1909 Haynes auto advertisement, already emphasizing female driving and the car's ability to tackle the rugged outdoors. Below: Early automobiles were not designed for the rugged Canadian landscape — an unknown car in Dawson, Yukon, sometime between 1903 and 1906.

made car ownership and use a *right* for average people on both sides of the border.

But America's proximity also hindered Canada's own industrial development. For many Canadians, it made little sense to build their own indigenous auto industry when American innovations, capital, technologies and firms could easily and quickly leap over any protective policies that might be erected to foster a national industry. Canada gained from the early and ubiquitous use of Henry Ford's Model T but lost any chance to create its own auto industry legacy, at least when it came to the production of Canadian-designed cars by Canadian-owned firms. There were a few Canadian auto firms, but virtually all of these died out by the time of the Great Depression.

Nonetheless, Canadians did succeed in the automotive world. Even though the Canadian sector was made up largely of branch plants, the industry became the most important sector of

economic activity in the country by the 1920s. Still, the American influence was always present as Canadians adapted and framed their industrial policy to take full advantage of the continental ties that had emerged in the industry over the decades. By the mid-1960s, the American connection had been solidified through a treaty, the Auto Pact, which forever tied Canada's industry

The car opened up a whole new world of travel, tourism and exploration. Driving through the big hollow tree in Stanley Park, Vancouver, 1923.

Sam McLaughlin, founder of General Motors of Canada, about 1925.

to that of the United States.

The pervasiveness of the American influence was also seen in the way the Canadian landscape was so dramatically altered through the car. After the 1920s, roadside culture in North America was similar in its many shapes, sounds and appearances. Yet it was not entirely an American theme. There were important Canadian variations. From the similar yet slightly different gas stations (eventually Esso in Canada, Exxon in the United States), drive-ins and drive-thrus (McDonald's versus Tim Horton's) and auto-oriented strip malls

and plazas (more often with covered parking in Canada, owing to the weather, of course), the two countries were each familiar with a shared automotive experience.

If the commonality of North American life was first and foremost a story shaped by the car, this was particularly true of the changes to society wrought by the automobile. Canadians and Americans shared similar experiences that were either created or changed by the car's arrival. The daily rituals of home and work were just as affected as the special moments that marked the passage of their lives. Coming of age, dating, weddings, children and death were all accompanied in some way by the automobile. Again, there might have been slight differences in these experiences across the continental divide (and across and within countries and regions too), but the automobile's impact upon society was undeniable.

While the Canadian auto story was unquestionably tied to its continental heritage, it also expressed its uniqueness through a nationalistic flair. In the beginning, there was a lively effort to manufacture an all-Canadian car. Gray-Dort, Russell, Canadian Car and a number of other manufacturers all tried to carve out a patriotic slice of the nascent car market. Though these efforts might not have lasted, the young Canadian car-parts industry did well and flourished under the Auto Pact regime. If there is a Canadian success story in the auto industry, it is surely in the parts sector, where a number of Canadian firms are among the best in the world.

During the wars, particularly during the Second World War, the Canadian auto industry pursued patriotism with zeal. The war effort was one that again reflected both the nationalism and the continentalism of the auto sector and its reach. While Canadian manufacturers were fighting the war by building cars, trucks and armoured vehicles, there was no denying that these were companies owned by American corporations. Canada had its own arsenal of democracy, but it was one that had much in common with the wartime efforts south of the border.

Eventually, even though in peacetime Canadians may have built American-designed Fords, Chevrolets and Chryslers in Windsor, Oshawa and Oakville, they often did so with important differences, attaching particularly Canadian attributes to models and giving them distinctive Canadian names (the Acadian, Laurentian, Montcalm, Rideau). A Canadian Ford Model T might come with a slightly different engine, or better headlights, or heavier upholstery (again, for the weather, of course). Early McLaughlin-Buicks were known for their better comportment and manufacture. Then there were the Canadian-built Studebakers, Volvos and Bricklins, all with uniquely Canadian stories.

Canadian car nationalism came in other forms too. In British Columbia and the Maritimes, drivers were not so quick to give up their own ways, as the colonial legacy of left-hand drive cars and driving on the left-hand side of the road stubbornly held out into the 1920s. Likewise, royal tours were a chance for Canadians to express their pride in their monarch and in the Canadian-built cars they were paraded in. For many Canadians and their families, the cross-country road trip on the Trans-Canada Highway (completed 1962) became a source of both myth and nostalgia. The Canadian Auto Workers union,

Early cars were open to the elements. At top, an ad for a 1909 Franklin; below, a 1903 Redpath.

which assembles the majority of cars in this country, remains the largest and most powerful in Canada, and its most nationalistic. Car racers such as the late Gilles Villeneuve, his son Jacques and Paul Tracy became household names and national heroes as they sped along the road tracks and ovals of the racing world.

All these expressions of nationalism were tempered by the global realities of the automobile and its industry. Canadians understood that both the nationalism and continentalism of their connections to the car were framed within a global context. The automobile was a product and process that shaped the world beyond Canada and North America. It also reached out from the rest of the world to shape Canada too.

This two-way street could be seen most prominently in the automotive industry. Even in the 1920s, Canadians exported hundreds of thousands of cars around the world, to exotic locales such as Malaysia and New Zealand. There, the need and desire for the car was just as great as it was in Canada. Car buyers around the world ensured that Canadians had jobs and a high standard of living. Car builders in Canada sought to ensure that Canadian-made cars could withstand the rigours of motoring from the rugged topography of Australia and South Africa, to India and places in between.

More recently, the global connectedness of

A 1947 Ford Monarch, illustrating the dramatic changes in car style and design in less than half a century.

the car industry has made Canadians realize how tied they are to trends, fads and events around the world. A decline in home prices in the United States might lead to a loss in consumer confidence and the layoff of thousands of auto workers in Oshawa or Windsor. The booming auto industries of China, Korea and India threaten the livelihood of small-town Canada, where parts companies such as Magna International (Aurora, Ontario) or Linamar Gear (Guelph, Ontario) have developed their expertise and maintain many of their plants. Environmental regulations and pressures, mandated from Kyoto to Washington, have a direct effect upon firms and workers in places such as British Columbia, a hotbed of the burgeoning fuel cell industry.

Yet these recent global connections are the story of the car's future in Canada. To fully comprehend the impact of the auto upon this country, one must start at the beginning. We need to go back in time, to the age before cars, when it was slowly but surely dawning upon Canadians that a revolution was brewing. A new machine was approaching, one that would utterly transform the people and their places.

A Ford Model S, the precursor to the phenomenally successful Model T.

The Auto Revolution Begins: Invention and Industry

A Model T takes to the road. The car would change the world forever.

At the end of the nineteenth century, Canadians knew a revolution was coming. Canada was still a young country, and many Canadians remembered well the celebrations that had accompanied Confederation in 1867. In 1900, the Dominion remained largely the same as it had been when a strapping John A. Macdonald became the new nation's first prime minister: Canada was still very rural, very colonial and very much the rugged and beautiful land that would later be romanticized in Hollywood films and on picturesque postcards.

Quite suddenly, on long dusty roads or in small quiet towns, Canadians saw the signs — and, even before that, heard the rumblings — of a new age, something unlike anything they had experienced. In 1901, as Canadians mourned the loss of their Queen, automobiles first appeared, a jarring signal that marked the end of Her Majesty's Victorian age. Trundling down bumpy roads,

Canadian contributions: An old McLaughlin ad illustrates the transition from the firm's carriages to its cars.
At left, a McLaughlin-Buick, built in Oshawa using American schematics.

snapping, gurgling and spewing, automobiles were startling, more akin to some Frankenstein-like creature from the pages of a novel than an object belonging to the genteel and gentlemanly era of Sir Wilfrid Laurier.

At first, Canadians felt unsure about the dawn of automobility. Some argued that these "horseless carriages" were a threat not just to people and horses, but to an age-old way of life. In Prince Edward Island, the legislature banned all autos in 1908, regarding them as the antithesis of the province's pastoral island existence. Other Canadians probably wondered if this was just another fad, like the bicycle craze of the 1890s.

Could a *machine* actually replace the horse — a mode of transportation that stretched back through time immemorial? After all, the railroads had created their own transportation revolution in the last two generations and remade Canada in their own way, but the rails did nothing to alter personal mobility. In 1901, Canada was still in the midst of Laurier's Great

Wheat Boom, and people still needed horses, especially in a country where four-fifths of the population remained tied to the farm.

Yet the revolution came quickly, even in rural Canada. As sightings of these loud, sputtering and sometimes scarily out-of-control contraptions became more common, Canadians began to see the outlines of a radical new way of life. Cars promised to make their lives easier, faster, more productive and adventurous and romantic. A new-found freedom beckoned with the car, one that would profoundly alter the way Canadians saw themselves and their world. As the century turned, for many Canadians a wondrous glance at these mysterious new vehicles was nothing less than a tantalizing glimpse of the future.

Canadians were not the only ones mesmerized by the potential of the automobile. The emergence of the automobile as a technology in the late nineteenth and early twentieth centuries connected the Canadian experience to continental and global developments that led to the widespread acceptance of the auto. There was no single inventor of the automobile. Amazingly, basic car technology is essentially the same today as it was in 1900 (cars still use gas-powered engines and four air-inflated rubber tires) and is the result of innovations from around the world. As Canadians sought to take full advantage of the wonders of modernity that the automobile promised, they quickly understood that the age of the car was a truly global phenomenon.

The first known automobiles, and the beginnings of the auto industry, can be traced to Europe and America. In their earliest efforts, inventors explored steam engines, electric- and, ultimately, gasoline-powered internal combustion engines as a way to power self-propelled vehicles. In Germany, Carl Benz and Gottlieb

Above: A Model T restored to all its glory. Note the red colour — not all of Mr. Ford's cars came in black.

Below: A Ford Model R. Before his spectacular success, Ford's first two car companies failed, a fate not like many others in the industry.

Vintage cars could last for decades. Here, a pre-First World War model is filled at an Esso station, 1949.

Daimler took an early lead in engine technology. In France, Louis Renault made important gearbox and drivetrain innovations; and the Michelin brothers, Édouard and André, became leaders in rubber tires. Like Germany, France quickly embraced automobiles as an expression of the new *Zeitgeist* of the age (*garage*, for instance, is derived from the original French usage).

The successful European inventors focused on building high-end luxury vehicles, designed for the wealthy elites of the Gilded Age. In America, a multitude of aspiring automakers also crowded the auto market with models mostly for the rich, though a few sought to build cars for America's growing, teeming masses. Their names — Olds, Dodge, Ford and Chevrolet — come down to us as durable remnants of a bygone era. Keen

competition meant that a happy collision of European and American innovations fuelled the rise of machines on both sides of the Atlantic.

Canadians were also part of the worldwide effort to solve the problem of personal mobility. As early as 1867, farm-boy inventor Henry Seth Taylor of Stanstead, Quebec, built a working steam-powered carriage that he showed at local fairs. Taylor was not alone at the dawn of the auto age. Canadian tinkerers were legion: from Montreal to Vancouver, Canadian inventors built steam-, gasoline- and electric-powered conveyances. Most have disappeared into the mists of time, but a few are noteworthy. In Quebec, George Foss and Henri-Emile Bourassa built working gasoline-powered cars that were able to propel their makers over short distances.

A 1905 Ford Model K, one of the last luxury vehicles built by Ford before 1908. With the Model T, Ford would focus on building cars for ordinary people, not the elite.

Yet most of these efforts were intended to build a single car as experiment or for ego, not to sell cars commercially.

At this point in the automobile revolution, in 1903, there were just a few hundred cars in Canada (182 in Ontario, the most of any province in the Dominion). Some were the products of tinkerers such as Bourassa and Foss. Others had been imported from American firms in Michigan operated by early auto pioneers Ransom Olds, Henry Leland (the creator of the Cadillac) or Henry Ford. Many of these cars were expensive yet unreliable, often breaking down, and difficult to repair. Some only operated for short stretches at a time and had poor brakes or handling, or were susceptible to bad weather. Aspiring Canadian motorists, like their American counterparts, were keen to find a car that would solve the problems of early motoring. Aspiring Canadian automotive entrepreneurs were also keen to find a car to build and sell, one that would take advantage of the growing acceptance of cars,

solve the problems of pricing and durability and, perhaps, make them wealthy too.

If there is one individual who can be credited with ensuring that Canada partook in the great automotive revolution, it was Gordon McGregor. While he may have been Canada's greatest automotive pioneer, McGregor's contribution had more to do with good fortune than invention or innovation. In 1904, McGregor, the thirty-one-year-old scion of a wagon-making family in Walkerville, Ontario (adjacent to Windsor), came to the realization that the horseless carriage was no mere fad, but the future of transportation. Like so many other bustling Canadian auto entrepreneurs in this period, McGregor was fascinated by cars, and he puzzled over the best way to take advantage of an industry he was sure would change the world.

As luck would have it, the McGregor family's Walkerville Wagon Works was almost directly across the river from the booming Midwestern metropolis of Detroit. As the centre of the

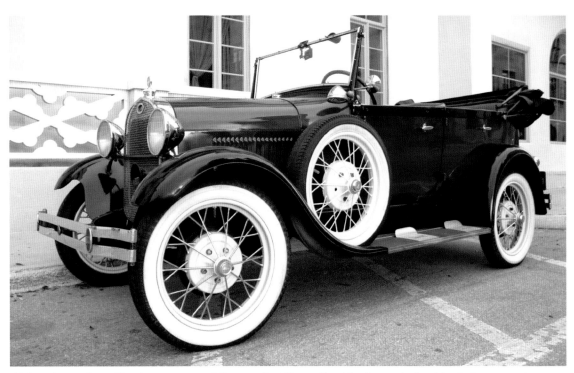

Before long, the utilitarian concept of the car that Henry Ford had popularized had given way to more stylistic offerings. Here a luxury car of the interwar period reflects the elegance of the automobile.

American wagon-building business, Michigan in the late nineteenth century had already become the heart of the burgeoning auto trade. McGregor was determined to get in on this business. In the summer of 1904, McGregor walked the streets of Detroit looking for partners to start some sort of auto enterprise. Knocking on various acquaintances' doors, he kept hearing the name of Henry Ford. Intrigued, McGregor tracked down Ford, who had already developed a reputation for technical prowess though his first two automobile ventures had ended in failure.

McGregor and Ford hit it off immediately. Ford liked McGregor's earnest approach and his willingness to take a chance on the Ford brand. McGregor was impressed by Ford's mechanical wizardry and his maniacal determination to build a practical car for the "common man." The two men came to an agreement: in exchange for 51 percent of Ford of Canada (the company was valued at $125,000), Ford and the American Ford Motor Company would provide McGregor with all the Ford schematics and production plans, and the right to sell and market Ford cars across the British Empire, save for the United Kingdom, which Ford kept for himself. This would allow Ford to leap the high tariff wall (35 percent) created by John A.'s National Policy on autos and take advantage of the lower Imperial tariff by having McGregor export cars from Canada. Once the tariff was added to imported vehicles, more expensive cars built by Ford in Canada cost slightly less than those from the United States; Fords exported from Canada to

Founding Ford of Canada in 1904, barely a year after its parent firm's creation, Gordon McGregor pioneered the Canadian automotive industry. Right, a model of a two-door Model T.

other British colonies also cost less than those exported directly from America because of the Imperial tariff. At the time, this seemed like a fair deal — after all, Ford itself had only been capitalized for $28,000 and was just one of dozens of carmakers in the Detroit area, most of which were barely afloat.

In 1904, the automobile industry in Canada was no sure thing. Car companies came and went: nearly five hundred had started in the United States between 1900 and 1908 and barely half survived. McGregor himself walked the streets of Windsor trying to sell Ford of Canada shares, and he was often met with disdain for what many considered a grubby, dangerous product. One prominent Walkerville lawyer avoided McGregor socially until he was finally cornered and convinced to invest $5,000, which he considered a donation to McGregor personally,

as opposed to a sensible investment. When the famous distilling Walker family, the town's namesake, discovered that an enterprising company employee had purchased Ford of Canada shares, they were aghast, and simply gave the offending shares to the firm's chemist to get them off the books. But over the next four years, the Ford operations on both sides of the border managed to do reasonably well. It seemed to McGregor that Ford had found a solid formula for success — building cars not for the robber barons, but for average folk.

The Model T changed all that. Launched in 1908, the Tin Lizzie, as the car quickly came to be known, became the most important automobile of all time. Built for the masses, Ford pioneered an approach that utilized new production techniques to make the car as cheaply as possible. This ran counter to most car companies of the time, which aimed to build more expensive vehicles for higher profits. In Windsor, McGregor simply followed Ford's car blueprints and factory plans, albeit on a smaller scale.

And what a vehicle it was. As a truly global phenomenon, Henry Ford and his famous Model T have, of course, a special place in the story of the auto. Ford's role in Canadians' emerging love affair with the car is no less important. Sturdy, dependable and easy to

Model Ts were put to innumerable uses. A depot hack, Windsor, 1923. Below, Ford logo from a 1915 grille plate.

operate and fix, the Model T changed the auto industry forever. Soon priced at a fraction of most cars on the market ($850 in the United States, $975 for the roadster in Canada), the car quickly took hold of the public's imagination and their pocketbooks.

The Model T was the greatest agent of the auto revolution in Canada. The Windsor operation built less than a thousand Model Ts in 1908 but shipped six thousand two years later, and production exploded after that. In 1917, the company produced fifty thousand vehicles, and over the next ten years, Ford of Canada built nearly half a million cars. In 1926, a year before Model T production ceased in Canada, the company produced an astonishing one hundred thousand vehicles (in the United States, production had peaked at a spectacular two million in 1923).

To keep up with this fabulous demand, Ford of Canada expanded furiously, building a new plant in 1913 and another new facility in 1922, the largest industrial building in the British Empire. The Ford phenomenon was not exclusive to Windsor. The company built branch plants in Toronto, Winnipeg, Montreal, Regina, Calgary, Vancouver and Saint John. The Windsor plant shipped partially built Model Ts by rail to the satellite facilities, where they were put together quickly and distributed to the growing ranks of Ford dealers.

Ford's techniques revolutionized large-scale production, and ushered in a new era of manufacturing. The outdoor body drop at Ford's Highland Park factory, 1913.

All of this fantastic production was not solely for Canadians. Ford of Canada exported thousands of Model Ts to destinations all over the globe. Taking full advantage of the original deal with Henry Ford, McGregor and Ford of Canada set up wholly owned Ford subsidiaries in far-flung locales such as South Africa, Malaysia, Australia, New Zealand and India. As early as 1906, a quarter of Windsor's production was exported. At the dawn of the auto age, Canada's industry was already globally oriented. By the 1920s, nearly half of all Canadian-built cars were exported overseas.

Ford's success had an astonishing impact upon Windsor. The little hamlet where Ford of Canada's massive factories sprouted quickly became known as Ford City, Canada. With Ford booming, the period between 1904 and 1933 saw a host of car companies cluster in Windsor, as the town quickly became a magnet for other automakers, both Canadian and American. Firms such as the Canadian Commercial Motor Car Company, Dominion Motors, Maxwell-Chalmers and Studebaker all converged on the once-sleepy border town. By the beginning of the

First World War, Windsor had become Canada's undisputed Motoropolis.

Among the later arrivals on the Windsor auto industry scene was a company headed by Walter Chrysler, which took over the old Maxwell-Chalmers company in 1925. Chrysler, who had previously worked at General Motors and was known in the Detroit–Windsor corridor as something of a mechanical genius, started the Canadian branch of his new company just a few weeks after establishing his firm in Detroit. By 1929, the success of his cars had led to the opening of a new seventy-acre plant on the outskirts of Windsor. Chrysler, like Ford, would remain a cornerstone of the Canadian auto industry in Windsor for decades to come.

While Windsor was the sparkplug of the early Canadian auto industry, Toronto was another important site of homegrown automotive innovation. Perhaps the most successful carmaker in Toronto was also the maker of the most successful Canadian-produced and -owned vehicle. In 1905,

Thomas A. Russell, an ambitious young businessman, took command of the foundering Canada Cycle and Motor Company (CCM). Like other bicycle makers, CCM had attempted to get into the car business but with little success. By 1903, the company's Locomobiles and Ivanhoes — relatively under-powered steam and electric vehicles — had failed in the marketplace. Upon taking control of the company and renaming a branch of it after himself, Russell decided to pursue gasoline-powered vehicles. In 1905, the Russell Model A debuted, followed quickly by the even more successful Model B in 1906 and a move to an expanded plant in West Toronto from the original Yonge Street factory. By 1910, the company was known across the country for well-engineered, quality vehicles and offered a full range of autos.

Model Ts were shipped across Canada and around the world, often in "knocked-down" form for easier transport.
Left: an early Model T ad. So successful was the car that Henry Ford discontinued print advertising for years — the car sold itself.

Russell's success was also a product of his showmanship. He adored publicity and used stunts, such as a race between one of his cars and a yacht along Lake Ontario, to promote the company. He opened the first showroom in downtown Toronto, at the corner of Bay and Temperance Streets. Russell also pushed the nationalist angle in selling the vehicles, proclaiming his car a "Thoroughly Canadian Car: Canadian Labour, Canadian Material, Canadian Capital" — clearly in contrast to McGregor's American approach at Ford of Canada. Ironically, after 1910, Russell used an imported Knight engine from the United States. Until 1915, the company produced thousands of

A Toronto car company: The morning shift leaving the Russell Motor Car Co. plant at King and Duncan streets (the building still survives). At right, an advertisement for the successful Russell auto, though production would be discontinued by the First World War.

vehicles, quite a few of which were exported overseas to the United Kingdom, Australia and New Zealand.

Russell's was not the only Canadian attempt to build a successful production car. In Orillia, Ontario, J.B. Tudhope, like McGregor another former carriagemaker, established a car plant with the help of a $50,000 grant from the city council. Tudhope imported schematics from the successful American firm of EMF but built the cars entirely in his own shop without using foreign parts or components. After his American partner failed in 1912, Tudhope gamely continued to produce and sell cars but followed into bankruptcy the next year. Robert Gray of Chatham, Ontario, also went into the business, producing

twenty-six thousand Gray-Dort cars within ten years of the company's founding in 1915. Along with these indigenous efforts at auto assembly, a healthy parts-and-supply sector grew up, mostly in southwestern Ontario. The early Canadian parts industry included firms such as Canadian Motor Lamp Company, Dominion Forge and Steel Company and the Canadian Spring Company.

A story not unlike McGregor's Windsor tale was unfolding at the McLaughlin Carriage Works in Oshawa, east of Toronto. Founded in 1869, the McLaughlin establishment was the largest carriagemaker in the country. Like McGregor, young Sam McLaughlin was enthusiastic about the prospects of the automobile

23

and in 1907 persuaded his father's firm to branch out into the production of cars. The company's early success was built around a licensing agreement with an American firm, Buick, which supplied engines for their McLaughlins in 1908. This plan showed some initial success, and the company sold more than one thousand vehicles by 1914. Within a few years, however, McLaughlin realized that keeping pace with the latest auto innovations was too costly: he decided to sell the family firm to his friend Billy Durant, the legendary founder of General Motors. In 1918, McLaughlin Motor became General Motors Canada and would go on to become the largest and most successful automotive company in Canada. By the early 1920s, Oshawa vied with Windsor as Canada's automotive capital.

As Windsor and Oshawa continued to boom, the auto industry was quickly evolving in a new, competitive marketplace. The period up to 1920 had seen the emergence of hundreds of automaking entrepreneurs on both sides of the border. But after 1920, the competition had become cutthroat, and capital demands in the industry had grown immensely. Companies that could not build enough cars, did not have the technology, could not machine the necessary parts or lacked the funds to keep producing, innovating and developing new products quickly died off or were bought out.

Others, such as Russell, had focused on munitions production during the Great War and were unable to get back into the market when peace returned (his factory was eventually sold to the Willys-Overland company, which continued to produce cars at the site until the 1930s). The last Canadian maker, Gray-Dort, closed its doors in 1925. Dozens of American firms in Canada also went under in the early 1920s. By the end of the decade, only the Big Three of General Motors, Ford and Chrysler survived, along with a handful of independents such as Studebaker, Nash and Hudson. In Canada, the branch plants of these firms constituted virtually the entirety of the Canadian assembly sector.

Nonetheless, the auto industry flourished and became one of the greatest sources of employment in the rapidly industrializing country. Canadians came from all across the Dominion to work in Windsor's bustling industry. Young men from farms in southwestern Ontario were drawn to the sprawling plants, as were thousands of immigrants who had come to Canada during the great Laurier boom that saw Canada's population explode before the Great War. Ford of Canada was the most spectacular example of this growth. The company grew from 17 employees in 1904, to 118 in 1910, 565 in 1912, 1,045 in 1914 and 2,879 in 1916. By 1920, the company had more than four thousand workers and was the largest industrial enterprise in the British Empire.

At Mr. Ford's factories, as the locals referred to McGregor's gigantic complex, Poles, Slovaks, Ukrainians and a multitude of workers of other ethnicities intermingled with Canadians of British descent and with the Franco-Ontarians whose families had lived in Essex County since the 1700s. African Canadians, the descendants of escaped American slaves who had settled in counties adjacent to the border, usually had the dirtiest, lowest-paying — and sometimes the hottest — jobs working at the sweltering steel-producing foundries.

The work itself was unlike anything nineteenth-century Canadians could have imagined. Ford's utilization of the moving assembly line, and the scale required by the growth and complexity of auto production, profoundly changed the manner and meaning of work. The massive assembly line, pulsating with humanity yet inhumanly loud, reordered production techniques and reshaped time. The auto industry production lines soon became known worldwide as Fordism, or the

By the 1930s, Oshawa's General Motors was the biggest Canadian company. Above, the factory in Oshawa prior to the 1918 GM takeover — the McLaughlin Carriage Co. Limited.
Left: A 1924 McLaughlin Buick Touring Car.

American System. The only thing that mattered was the speed of the line, and all workers' actions quickly became measured down to the second. Experts in "time management," such as Frederick W. Taylor, spawned their own science, seeing human workers as little more than automatons, no different from the pulleys, conveyors or stamping machines of the factory.

Fordism and Taylorism meant the end of skilled labour on the assembly line. Nineteenth-century work had been predicated on craft and knowledge handed down through the centuries. Now the only thing that mattered was repetition of a single task, at one spot on the line, hundreds or thousands of times a day. Time took on new meaning as factories operated not on the predicates of craftsmanship, but on the tyranny of the shift, the clock and, above all else, the speed of the assembly line.

Still, with the end of the Great Wheat Boom, overcrowding of farms and the new realities of a waged economy, thousands of men came to Windsor or Oshawa to take part in the new industry. Though they may have developed camaraderie and might have maintained their ethnic or hometown ties when they started, the work was punishing. Turnover was a terrible problem at the large facilities, where the physical and psychological stress of the factory quickly became unbearable. For every three or four workers hired at Ford, only one lasted more than a few months. Company-sponsored associations, teams or social gatherings — corporate welfare — did little to staunch the turnover or to alleviate the growing discontent under the smokestacks.

Sensing the turmoil that was building in his growing workforce, Henry Ford was first to respond, and in doing so was lionized as a champion of the working man. In 1914, Ford shocked the world by announcing that, henceforth, his workers would receive $5 a day, a fantastic rate of pay that essentially doubled auto workers' wages. A year later, across the river, McGregor offered his own workers $4 a day. The effect of the new Ford policies was tremendous:

25

Thousands more men came to Windsor to try to get a job, absenteeism declined, as did turnover, and workers were happier and less inclined to agitate for unionization — for now.

More importantly, the new rate of pay dragged all auto workers' wages upward (to the displeasure of Ford's competitors) and made the car factory worker the envy of the working classes. This was the new definition of Fordism — by paying his employees so well, and thus spreading his spectacular wealth to thousands of families, Ford ensured that average workers could afford to buy his cars. This virtuous circle boosted the economy, made auto consumption affordable and kept the factories humming — for now. On both sides of the border, the auto industry, and Fordism, had created a new economic paradigm.

Thus, it is not surprising that the visible spread of the auto industry was not limited to the factories of carmakers. The impact of the effectiveness of the assembly line and the massive scale of the factories became the new way of

industry. Mass production became the standard in Canada not just in automobiles, but in virtually all other consumer industries, from canned foods to undergarments to tools. Service industries were also swept up by motordom: the sale and marketing of cars quickly became a big business, as important as the production of automobiles themselves. Automobiles became the staple of advertising, from magazines to newspapers to the new, fantastic medium of radio.

Even before the First World War, hundreds of Canadians had established car dealerships all across the nation. In Toronto, a veritable "auto row" grew up along Bay Street, north of City Hall. By the 1920s, there were thousands of dealerships in virtually every nook and cranny of the country, many of which are still in operation today. Auto shows were another popular way by which Canadian makers publicized and sold their wares. Auto shows became a staple at exhibitions, such as the Canadian National Exhibition in Toronto, the Calgary Stampede and the Regina Exhibition, and at venues all across the country.

The auto revolution's impact on work spread rapidly. From doctors to lawyers to farmers, the car completely altered how Canadians did their jobs and created thousands of new jobs too, from auto mechanics to delivery services to car washes to parking lots. At the end of the war, the car had recreated work and the economy in Canada.

By the 1920s, the first phase of Canada's automotive revolution was unquestionably in place. The cars, factories and workers of Canadian motordom had already reshaped work, industry, the economy and the sights and sounds of Canadian transportation. Now, town, country and the rest of society would quickly fall under the sway of the automobile.

Studebaker's huge Hamilton plant, 1940s. The company took over a wartime munitions factory.

TWO

Canada's New Carscape:
Town and Country Remade

In 1912, Jack Haney began the trip of a lifetime. A twenty-three-year-old mechanic from St. Catharines, Ontario, Haney was about to embark on a fifty-two-day automobile tour across Canada with British travel writer Thomas W. Wilby. Starting in Halifax, the two men drove their 1912 Reo Special Touring Car nearly seven thousand kilometres across a country that had, at the time, barely eighteen kilometres of paved road. Haney and Wilby rumbled down dirt roads, through cities and towns, up and down hills and mountains, on rails and across some of the toughest and most unforgiving terrain in the world. The success of their journey garnered newspaper headlines in every Canadian city and town

Above: Thomas W. Wilby, Jack Haney and their Reo "Pathfinder" on their journey from Halifax to Vancouver, 1912.
Left: A 1919 Reo.

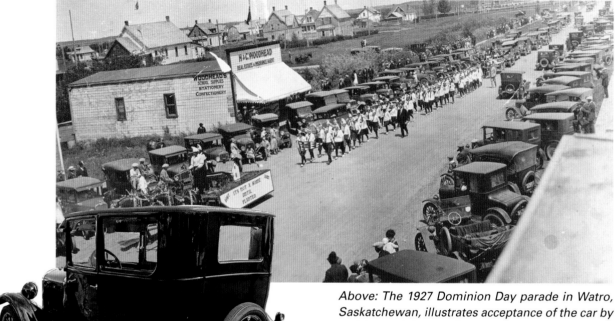

Above: The 1927 Dominion Day parade in Watro, Saskatchewan, illustrates acceptance of the car by residents of the province.
Left: A 1925 Model T — the new workhorse of the farm, and a symbol of agricultural prosperity.

through which they passed, and became the stuff of motoring legend.

The landscape Haney and Wilby travelled across would be unimaginable to Canadians today. It wasn't just that there were no paved roads. There were virtually no place signs along the way, few traffic signs and certainly no traffic lights. There was none of the roadside culture that permeates the Canadian landscape today: no gas stations, drive-thrus, car dealerships, car washes, parking lots, parking garages, highways and ramps. Tim Horton would not be born for another eighteen years, and the first coffee shop to bear his name would not appear in Hamilton, Ontario, for another half-century.

Yet Haney and Wilby's trip was more than just a tourist tale. Their journey symbolized a moment of profound transformation. Proving that a car could travel across Canada, the two men showed that Canadians were no longer separated by their forbidding geography. In stitching together this vast nation in their sturdy Reo, Haney and Wilby's trip changed Canada every kilometre that they drove. Canadians could now go anywhere they wished and could connect to their country, and with one another, in a manner that horse and rail had never allowed them. Canada's landscape was now an open tableau, a new "carscape" that was the manifestation of what motordom's revolution had wrought upon the young Dominion.

This transformation was apparent a scant fifteen years later, during Canada's 1927 Diamond Jubilee. At celebrations, parades, picnics and fireworks displays across the country (there had been none during the difficult wartime fiftieth anniversary in 1917), Haney and Wilby would have been struck by the sheer ubiquity of the automobile and its influence upon the landscape. Cars had remade virtually every aspect of life and had emerged as a symbol and agent of Canadian modernity.

Perhaps most profoundly evident was the new sense of freedom — to travel, to work, to worship, to celebrate, to just go anywhere at anytime — that seemed to permeate Canadians' relationship with the car. The great barriers of distance, space and time, which the railroads had only partially overcome, seemed to vanish for average Canadians. The inexpensive cars of Windsor and Oshawa meant that Canadians were empowered in a way they had never been before.

The spread of the car, and the freedom it represented, was astonishing. In 1912, when Haney and Wilby made their trip, there were just over twenty thousand cars in Canada. By the end of the Roaring Twenties, a decade that owed its name more to the automobile than anything else, Canadians owned more than one million cars, and nearly half of all Canadian families owned a car. The Fordist model, which drove down prices and boosted pay, allowed thousands of Canadians to buy cars: by the mid-1920s, the Model T was half its original price. Car ownership was also made quick and convenient by innovations pioneered by the auto industry that redefined consumerism. Auto financing, which emerged with the creation of the General Motors Acceptance Corporation in Canada in 1919, provided a new means of financing car purchases and allowed Canadians to spread the cost of their automobile over time. After the Great War, the freedom of the automobile was

Notwithstanding Ford's utilitarian efforts, automobiles quickly came to epitomize and reinforce class distinctions.

Markets became an intersection between city and country, auto and pre-auto. Ottawa's Byward Market illustrates this collision of rural and urban, horse and machine, 1918.

achieved by many Canadians with only a few easy instalment payments.

Paradoxically, at the same time that the car held out the vast possibility of freedom for Canadians, it placed new-found constraints upon them as well. Licensing and registration meant a new invasive relationship between Canadians and their governments. Traffic rules, signs and policing constrained their behaviour and subjected them to a whole new set of laws. Freedom to drive wherever, yes, but the state's long arms now had a new way to regulate Canadians' activities. At the same time, while the Model T may have liberated the common man (and woman), by the 1920s, cars represented the same old class distinctions and the same old

social hierarchy. Wealthy Canadians drove their expensive cars, while less well-off Canadians were relegated to the modest Tin Lizzie or Chevy. Within a few years, the automotive "price ladder" announced Canadians' position in the social pecking order even before they stepped out of their cars.

Moreover, Canadians could now travel across their vast land, but in doing so, they and their cars began a process that threatened to make the landscape a generic, never-ending filmstrip of roadside repetition, and little more. The virus-like spread of the automobile and its supporting infrastructure meant a certain sameness over the landscape: Canadians might be able to travel all over the country in their cars, but the same Ford

dealerships, Esso stations and junkyards graced every corner of Canada and threatened, in time, to erase any notion of local distinctiveness.

Then there was the impact upon the auto towns. Before the First World War, the car had had its greatest impact upon the automotive cities of Windsor and Oshawa, where the noisy, smoking factories grew to their sprawling sizes. During the war, when the industry had turned its attention to building *matériel* for the Canadian and Allied forces overseas, the car's impact had been somewhat slowed. But the end of hostilities in 1918 meant the return of veterans, and the return of full-blown production. Soon, cars were being churned out in the tens of thousands, the majority of which were shipped to the growing metropolises of the country.

In cities, where cars proliferated in increasing numbers after the war, the change was dramatic. Streets that had once been the domain of horse and buggy quickly gave way to the motor car, which made work and life so much faster, more convenient and *modern*. The buzz of a thousand autos represented progress for many Canadians, and car-clogged cities became the epitome of Canada's new-found industrial, economic and political maturity. By the jubilee year of 1927, the first automatic

Above: Cars allowed people to travel with an ease and range previously unimaginable. Picnicking at "Little Arm," Valeport, Saskatchewan, 1920.
Right: Street signs became a necessary and ubiquitous aspect of the Canadian landscape because of cars.

The horrific toll of thousands of car accidents was a terrible consequence of so many cars on Canadian roads. Below: A Model T tire; its spokes were originally made of wood.

traffic lights had replaced police officers at fifteen intersections in downtown Toronto, and more would soon come. The next year, Vancouver got its first automated traffic light. By the end of the decade, automobile traffic had become one of the defining aspects of modern urban life.

Of course, the modernity of the car brought its own problems. Whereas city dwellers once had complained of mountains of excrement and decaying horse corpses, in the new era, traffic increased, parking became difficult and the belching, loud, smoking engines of cars (most commonly Henry Ford's Model T Flivvers) were another form of pollution; unexpected, unwelcome and as pervasive as the cars themselves. Oil leaks, breakdowns, discarded tires and the cacophony of confusion over who had "the right of way" led to conflict and collision in the streets, which often overwhelmed newcomers to the city.

More troublesome was the increase in accidents and the number of children and pedestrians killed on city roads as cars and people jockeyed for ownership of the street. In 1921, 197 Canadians were the victims of traffic fatalities. By 1929, that figure had reached 1,300. This loss could never compare to the horror visited by the Great War and the influenza pandemic, which had claimed thousands of Canadians. But in an era of peace, the seemingly senseless loss of life — especially of children — to cars was loudly condemned. In cities and towns across the nation, parents, politicians and pedestrians called out for some sort of control over the motor car and fought to claim the street as their own. Some advocated banning cars outright from certain streets or areas or pushed to slow speed limits to a crawl. But by then the car was ensconced, its presence permanent. Instead of fighting the car itself, cities attempted to curtail its excesses, boosting policing, creating traffic signs and promoting good driving campaigns, all of which did little. Notwithstanding the ongoing carnage of the roads, within decades city streets were almost entirely given over to the auto.

The vast number of cars that quickly clogged Canadian city streets also brought the city-shaping infrastructure of the automobile. Roads, tunnels, intersections, curbs and medians needed to be rebuilt to meet the carscape's needs, and city

A rather bizarre postcard from 1910 depicts "The Modern Farmer." One can only assume that the idea was to express the importance of the auto for getting product to market. Right: An elaborate hood ornament from a Model T.

fathers hastened to accommodate society's newest, grandest pacesetter. Street corners, which before the car had always been square, were cut into curves to reflect the automobile's ability to sweep around a corner. Construction — for the huge car dealerships, parking lots, car washes, service stations and garages — also added to the roar of the Twenties. In places such as Calgary, London or Saint John, cars and their accoutrements redefined main streets and town centres. By the time of the 1929 stock-market crash, Toronto's Bay Street had become synonymous not only with high finance, but with the grip of the auto upon the cityscape.

If the city was the epicentre of motordom's dramatic makeover, its impact was no less felt upon Canada's great rural heartland. Farmers were among the automobile's leading advocates; cars made farm life so much easier and gave rural Canadians a mobility they could have only dreamt about in the nineteenth century. Motorized tractors also became a staple of farm life by the end of the decade, but it was the Model T that revolutionized rural living.

Model Ts became as common as barns on the Canadian Prairies and were indispensable to agriculturalists as a tool, a lifeline to the wider world and a sign of their regional distinctiveness. Saskatchewan had the highest rate of ownership in the country in the early 1920s, and Ottawa's automobile tariff, designed to protect central Canadian manufacturers, became a sore point for progressive Western farmers, who were the most enthusiastic auto buyers and the leading *demandeurs* of free trade. By the mid-1920s, the cost of cars for farmers was a key election issue and a growing indication of Western discontent. By then, farmers felt that a car was no longer a luxury, but a necessity. Farmers argued they should be able to buy cars at the cheapest prices — even if it meant buying a Model T from just across the border instead of from Windsor. In Ottawa, their arguments made little headway, and the tariff remained intact even after changes in 1926.

As it was increasingly accepted in cities and on farms, the car began to reconnect the space between the town and country in new ways. Markets became an early site of rural-urban auto intersection, a place that was at once part of both Canada's old agricultural heritage and its motorized, modern future. From the dusty town squares of the Western provinces to the old urban meeting spots of Ontario and Quebec and the Maritimes, markets illustrated the ability of the auto to redefine social geography. Horses and modern horsepower mixed in an uneasy understanding as farmers melded the old ways with the new technologies to hawk their wares and learn the latest news. At marketplaces — Canadians' meeting places for centuries — the car represented both change and continuity.

Farmers led the charge to improve roads across the country so they could take their crops to market and get to the city. But savvy governments also pushed for road improvement. In the 1920s and 1930s, municipal and provincial demands to provide tourists (mostly American) with a way to get to Canadian places (to spend their dollars!) triggered the first great wave of road and highway building. By the mid-1920s, Ontario, Canada's most auto-intensive province, was building three hundred kilometres of highways a year, largely to attract American auto travellers. Construction boomed all across the country, as provinces (responsible for road-building) hastened to take advantage of the influx of wealthy visitors. From the breathtaking Rocky Mountain roads leading to Banff, to the Queen Elizabeth Way in southern Ontario, to the Cabot Trail in Cape Breton, auto tourists poured into and across the nation.

Roads were also built to open up "cottage country," giving new meaning to Canadians' sense of their country and to their notions of leisure time. While the rails had first helped to "colonize" the hinterlands of

Cars from the 1920s and 1930s are sought-after and sometimes modified collectors' items. Here a 1931 Ford has been "souped up."

northern Ontario and Quebec, now the car could take all Canadians easily to what was seen increasingly as the vacationland of the carscape. Destinations such as the Sunshine Coast, Muskoka, Mount Tremblant and the Gatineaus were now, thanks to the car, no longer exclusively for the rich. A new subculture was born as cars became synonymous with cottages and weekends away. Like markets, cottage country came to represent the intersection of Canada's wilderness past and its modern present. The vehicle of modern-day *voyageurs*, the car allowed enjoyment of the wild without the risk and inconvenience that had previously made travelling the Canadian landscape so difficult and dangerous.

Yet one did not have to travel far, or to some exotic, hitherto inaccessible, destination to enjoy the fruits of auto travel. Canadians, especially from cities, used their cars for simple, quick and happy excursions to the near-wilderness that bordered so many towns and cities. The definition of recreation was quickly altered to include the

The automobile made Canada a major vacation destination. A car at Jasper, Alberta, 1950s.

automobile. The 1920s was the era of the getaway, and Canadians piled into their cars to go picnicking, camping or to make their country one gigantic backyard. Chevys, Chryslers, Flivvers, Dorts, Russells and Buicks all became moving caravans, providing couples, families, lovers and those wishing to escape the tyranny of the train schedule the freedom to "park" just about anywhere they wished. In doing so, they blurred the differences between city and country, annexing them to the rule of the automobile with each pit stop along the road.

With better roads and highways came signage, which literally labelled the Canadian landscape. With the mass mobility offered by cars, tourists and travellers now had to know where "there" was, and place and space were given new meaning as cars conditioned Canadians to know where

Parades and patriotism: Mounties and a Royal Visit to Niagara Falls, 1951.

sented by a uniquely Canadian problem: on which side of the road were cars driven? Reflecting its mixture of French, British and American influences, Canadians drove on different sides of the road, depending upon where they lived. In British Columbia and the Maritime provinces (and in Newfoundland, which did not join Confederation until 1949), motorists followed the British practice of driving on the left side. In Quebec and Ontario (and the Prairies, which were largely populated by Upper Canadians and Americans), the practice was to follow the old French system, or the American, of driving on the right side.

These local differences could not survive the carscape's relentless expansion, as the experience in British Columbia demonstrates. At the dawn of the auto age, Canada's westernmost province retained the steadfastly *British* adjective of its name with pride. Logically following the motherland's example, BC motorists drove on the left side of the road. By 1913, there were seven thousand cars in the province. Yet the thousands of automobile tourists that came to BC every year, mostly from the United States, were often confused by the different rules of the road. Debate raged for some time, with many British Columbians expressing the belief that changing to the predominantly (North) American right-hand drive was disloyal to the Crown. Eventually, however, the desire for uniformity prevailed, and in 1922 legislation passed mandating all drivers to shift to the right. By 1924, the last holdout, Prince Edward Island, had switched as well (though it limited the car's use on the island). Ironically, Canadian car factories, such as Ford of Canada in Windsor, continued to build right-hand drive for British colonial export markets, even after driving on the left was prohibited in Canada.

While the immobility and isolation of the nineteenth century quickly gave way to the automotive freedom of the twentieth century,

they were and where they were going. No longer was geographic knowledge local — motor travellers had signs to take them where they wanted to go. Nineteenth-century localism and isolation quickly disappeared with the appearance of road signs and directions, which connected and contextualized towns, hamlets, villages and outposts across the Canadian carscape's vast expanse.

The end of localism was perhaps best repre-

Motorsports mania: An auto race at the Central Canada Exhibition, Ottawa, 1925. Below, an early Mercedes race car.

cars also challenged Canadians' long-held notions of societal norms. The rituals of everyday life were soon subsumed by the car. Weddings, funerals, church attendance and a thousand other public (and private) human moments became unimaginable without the car. Courtship was also changed. Young couples were no longer confined to their parents' front porch to flirt but were free to cavort unchaperoned, in city or in town, in their best impression of Twenties' icons Zelda and F. Scott Fitzgerald. The car gave young couples their own private space, away from prying eyes. The back seat of the car became more than just some space for extra luggage, to the consternation of a few disapproving Canadians.

Automobiles soon became a part of Canadians' pomp, pageantry and patriotism as well. Commemoration and celebration were well served by the car, from Dominion Day parades, to Royal Tours, to the mourning of brothers, sons and fathers lost in the Great War. Canadians loved to see and to be seen in cars, and they took any opportunity to put their cars (and themselves) on display. It became a new rite of passage for Canadians to have their photos taken in, on, beside — or under — their cars. From prime ministers to workers on Labour Day, cars on parade assumed a central place in Canadian public expression, and continue to do so.

Cars were a centrepiece of exhibitions and parades and an attraction in their own right. The 1920s was a decade of fads, and the automobile was the greatest fad in history. Car races — on land, on ice, for speed, for distance, for endurance — became a staple amusement across the country. The newest models were on display at the latest exhibitions and fairs, and the largest fair of all, the Canadian National Exhibition, even had the grand, permanent Automotive Building built on its grounds in 1929.

The car's impact on societal norms went much deeper than fads or pageantry. Again, American influences spilled over into Canada. In his titanic battle with Henry Ford, General Motors' chief Alfred Sloan redefined the auto industry by introducing a "price ladder" of vehicles "for every purse and purpose," from Cadillac, at the top of the ladder, down to Chevrolet, for the economy-conscious. Just as importantly, Sloan emphasized styling in his cars, focusing on curves and colours, which changed annually. Compared to the static, ancient-looking and seemingly always black Model T, there was no contest. By the end of the decade, GM was on top, both in the United States and Canada, where Oshawa followed Sloan's directives. Ford and Chrysler, in Detroit and Windsor, were left to try to catch up by mimicking The General, introducing new brands of their own and following the new auto reality. Soon Ford had Lincoln, while Chrysler had Plymouth.

Sloan's new rules of the automobile industry did not just topple the Model T and the idea of a car for practical purposes only; it marked a sea change in branding and social consciousness and the very notion of "newness" in society. All this was achieved through advertising, which bombarded Canadians with images of status and adventure. Advertising took on a whole new dimension because of the auto industry. In the 1920s, colour was added to magazine advertising, supplementing newspapers and, of course, radio, as the mainstays of carmakers' efforts. The new ads showed daring drivers tackling wilderness landscapes and femme fatales throwing automotive caution to the wind. The automobile and its advertisements became the new dream-makers of a generation and set in place ideas and images of self and society that remain today.

With Sloan's new conception of the car and its connection to social standing, the automobile became the outward expression of class differences. From limousines down to lowly Model Ts, nothing expressed a person's status quite like his or her car. Brands such as Cadillac or Chevy became shorthand for their drivers' stations in life, and Henry Ford's notion of a classless, utilitarian Model T was washed away in a wave of car-consciousness that remains today — the Doozy, or Duesenberg, became a part of everyday vocabulary and an expression of magnificence.

Canadians knew that royalty was chauffeured in only the best cars: When His Highness George VI and his bride, Queen Elizabeth (the Queen Mum), embarked on their trip across Canada in 1939 (the first reigning monarch to visit the country), they did so in a Royal Buick, built at General Motors' Oshawa plant in honour of the occasion. The Royal Tour represented a perfect example of the intersection of cars, class and corporatism. As the motorcade passed, thousands of Canadians turned out to cheer on the royal couple, cheering on, too, General Motors and its luxury brand, Buick.

The impact of automobiles upon shifting societal norms was apparent in the images — and realities — of Canadian women and the car. Canadians' quick acceptance of the car coincided with women's victory in the fight between 1917 and 1924 to vote federally and across most of the country. The liberation of women politically was accompanied by their new-found expression of freedom through driving. Cars were advertised specifically for women, and when the self-starter and the closed body revitalized engineering and design in the 1920s, women became among the most visible enthusiasts of motoring. Like the speakeasies and gangsters of Prohibition, or the go-go greed of the stock market bubble, the Twenties flapper and her car became icons of the decade on both sides of the border.

Cars exploded the nineteenth-century notions of separate spheres and strict Victorian bearing for Canadian women. While the female motorist increasingly began to appear on university campuses, at coffee houses and on the well-travelled tourist highways and byways of the

Increasingly stylish automobiles quickly became mechanical works of art, with their own auto shows, advertising and hierarchy of brands.

country, not all Canadian women took part in this mechanized free-for-all. Some women could not afford an automobile, or were not expected to drive, and certainly not expected to repair or service their cars. Others felt that women should not even have driver's licences, as it was "unwomanly" to operate a car, though this notion was quickly dismissed as unfair or impractical: another example of the car's quiet impact on equality. Yet notions of a "gentler sex" persisted: a further demonstration of how the automobile's promise of freedom was entangled with reminders of the old constraints. Women could drive, yes, but their

The battleground: Cars and street-cars struggle for supremacy near Vancouver's Granville Station, circa 1927.

allow the car complete freedom over their roadways and restricted its use. Many Canadians resented the polluting, noisy impact of the car upon street and country road and its invasion of the pristine wilderness of park and mountain. Some felt the car destroyed acceptable notions of womanhood, courtship and manners; others hated the car for the carnage it had visited upon family, friends and neighbours. Unquestionably, all Canadians recognized the amazing change that the auto had brought in what seemed like the blink of an eye.

The car drove on, powered by Gordon McGregor, Jack Haney and a million other Canadians who loved what the car represented, paradoxes and all. For a young, brash nation, the period before the liberating arrival of the car was tainted by unhappy events, including the Great War, the 1919 Winnipeg General Strike and the influenza pandemic of 1918–1920. In the glow of the 1920s, where the car reigned supreme, the modern future that the car represented seemed endless and amazing. Little did Canadians know that the reign of the automobile was about to be interrupted. Before it became absolute, the carscape's advance would face its own roadblocks, the twin challenges of Depression and War.

driving was still viewed through the lens of traditional male-female roles.

By the end of the Roaring Twenties, the car's grip upon Canadians was almost complete. Town and country had been remade, as had the ideals, rituals and notions of self and society. In some places, remnants of a Canadian way of life predating the car continued to resist the relentless spread of the auto. In a few cities, street railways continued their uneasy coexistence with the car. Some provinces were much more reluctant to

THREE

Canadian Motordom in Depression and War

George Burt was born in 1903, just at the dawn of the auto age. Growing up in Toronto, Burt was too young to participate in the First World War. After the war, he followed his father, a bricklayer, into the trades, becoming a plumber. During the Roaring Twenties, Burt worked here and there — positions were easy to come by then. Serendipitously, in 1929, Burt got a good job as a welder at the big General Motors plant in Oshawa. This was just before the Great Crash, and the same year that the Detroit–Windsor Tunnel linking the two cities was opened to auto traffic. Little did Burt know that things would change so quickly. Little did he know either that the rest of his life would be affected by his job in the auto industry or that the economic insecurity he would experience in the long, miserable decade called the Dirty Thirties would shape the lives of thousands of auto workers.

Life was hard for Burt and his family during the Depression, as it was for millions of Canadians. GM, like most other carmakers, laid off workers during slowdowns. When work was good, the line sped up, forcing Burt and his fellow workers to maintain a back-breaking pace or lose their jobs. With the downturn in the economy, their pay was cut — a far cry from the glory years when Ford had instituted its $4 day at Windsor. Back then,

Cadillac, 1935: The Great Depression challenged even the most luxurious brands, and that year even Cadillac cut their prices.

The struggle over unionization took place in the auto industry's giant factories, such as Ford's works in Windsor. Above: A UAW pin from the 1937 strikes.

things were good for auto workers. No longer. At one point, Burt was nearly forced to go on relief, a mark of shame for his family, and an indication of how far things had fallen from the boom times in the industry.

The difficulties Burt faced profoundly influenced his experience and the experiences of many other Canadians from the 1930s to the 1950s. Burt decided, like thousands of other men in the Canadian auto industry, to fight back. In 1937, Burt joined a union drive at Oshawa and was one of the founders of Local 222 of the fledgling United Auto Workers (UAW), an American union that had come to Canada. It was a risky decision. The Big Three of GM, Ford and Chrysler fought the union tooth and nail, and it took years to gain security, rights and recognition for auto workers such as Burt and his fellows on the line. But Burt proved to be good at organizing and fighting for workers' rights. In no time at all, he became secretary of his local, then was

elected director of the Canadian branch of the UAW, where he had a prominent vantage from which to understand the dramatic ups and downs that followed the car and its industry for the next thirty years.

For every boom, there is usually a bust. In the nearly three decades after Gordon McGregor visited Henry Ford in Detroit to make a deal for a car company, the auto and its industry had swept across Canada like a revolution. The carscape that had been created had remade virtually every aspect of Canadian life. But the Depression, and the war that followed it, threatened to push the automobile from its perch as Canada's most pervasive influence. The economic downturn essentially knocked the world off its wheels, while the war literally ended automotive production. Yet the automobile and its industry would persist, and by 1950, the car had reclaimed its crown, in no small part due to the hard work of men such as Burt and his fellow workers.

The car became a symbol — and a symptom — of the problems of the Great Depression, particularly for urban workers and farm families.

The amazing growth in the auto industry from the beginnings of McGregor's Ford Windsor operation in 1904 was itself a cause of the Depression. While the 1929 stock market crashes on Bay and Wall Streets garnered all the headlines, the economic slowdown was, in part, due to industrial overcapacity. This overcapacity was caused by the very Fordist technological advances that had seen the auto sector make such astounding leaps forward in production and efficiency. In the Canadian auto industry by the late 1920s, the auto factories at Windsor and Oshawa could easily produce four hundred thousand cars a year. But the highest Canadian demand in the 1920s had been for only two hundred and sixty thousand cars. When the downturn came, workers at Ford and Chrysler and GM became, like the cars they built, excess capacity.

By the time governments got around to doing anything about the Depression, the carscape that had flourished in the 1920s was in dire straits. There were still cars being built, and the vast changes in the physical landscape that the auto had brought were still prominent. But

A "Bennett buggy" — a car pulled by horses because the owner couldn't afford gas, repairs or tires — illustrated the depth of the Depression and the challenge to motordom.

Canadian motordom was in trouble. In the decade before 1929, Canadian auto factories regularly produced more than two hundred thousand vehicles a year. Some years, nearly half of these cars were exported around the world. In 1931, production plummeted to a meagre sixty-one thousand cars, less than ten thousand of which were exported.

Auto companies, which had been fabulously profitable before 1930, now faced spectacular losses. At Ford of Canada, losses were more than $5 million in 1932, assembly plunged to barely a third of what it had been in 1929 and the company's satellite plant in Montreal was shut down permanently. The problems were just as acute at GM and Chrysler. The industry as a whole, which employed twelve thousand workers in 1926, cut nearly a third of its jobs. Firms such as Reo, Studebaker and Packard closed their Canadian branch plants, in some instances for good.

This downturn wasn't like others in Canadian history. Along with creating the boom times, the auto industry had helped create a new kind of worker. The massive growth in the auto sector and its supporting industries (from parts production to the auto service industry) had, over the course of three decades, shifted the nature of work in Canada. Before the auto, the vast majority of Canadians worked as "hewers of wood or drawers of water" — as agriculturalists or in mining or forestry or a host of other extractive jobs.

By the Great Crash of 1929, Canadians were more likely to be part of an urban, working-class population dependent on waged labour in this new industrial economy, one represented by the automobile. In 1921, the Dominion Bureau of Statistics reported that the majority of Canada's people no longer lived on farms but in urban areas. The growth of places such as Windsor and Oshawa were a testament to the magnetism of auto jobs for Canadians, both newcomers and natives.

But when the economy went sour, and the factories closed, these newly unemployed people had nowhere to go, no way to survive. There was no farm to go back to, and without wages, there was no food. At the depths of the crisis, in 1933, one-quarter of non-farm workers were unemployed, and about one in five Canadians, or about two million people, were dependent on public handouts to survive. George Burt and his family were among these Canadians.

Of course, being on the farm during this period wasn't much better, as wheat prices fell and whole acres of farmland were swept away by a dustbowl of wind and soil degradation. The Tin Lizzies that had been such a source of help for farmers in the 1920s quickly came to symbolize the difficulties of the 1930s. Grasshopper infestation on the Prairies was so bad that one couldn't drive for more than a short while without having to stop the car and clean out all the dead grasshoppers clogging the grille and engine.

Cars symbolized the despair of the Depression in another way: the Bennett buggy. Named after millionaire Conservative Prime Minister R.B. Bennett, whose tenure coincided with the depths of the Depression, a *Bennett buggy* became the term across the country to describe an auto pulled by horses or oxen because the owner could not afford repairs, gas or tires. Bennett buggies, like Bennett blankets (newspapers covering men asleep on park benches) or eggs Bennett (broiled chestnuts), became shorthand for all that had gone wrong

Top: Young, unemployed workers trekked to Ottawa on the rails to demand that the government do something to help them. Bottom: A Ford Model T truck.

in the Canadian economy. Many Canadians simply couldn't afford to keep their cars. For the first time since the auto swept onto Canadian roads, the number of registered cars

In the depths of the Depression, the car was still essential. Department of National Defence trucks transporting men to work in a gravel pit, 1934.

dropped significantly, from more than 1.2 million to barely a million.

Cars were the face of the Depression in other ways too. The relief camps that sprouted up across the land as governments desperately tried to keep the masses of restless unemployed workers occupied used cars as a way to ferry men to and fro. Cars and trucks became the standard mode of transportation for work details in Canada's hinterland, from British Columbia to northern Ontario. So recently a destination for the carefree motorists of the Roaring Twenties, the rugged wilderness became a conveniently isolated place for governments to send thousands of potentially troublesome men.

These relief camps were also a sign of the lack of any concrete plan from government leaders as to what to do about the Depression. R.B. Bennett's suggestions came too little too late, while W.L. Mackenzie King, his Liberal successor (and predecessor), did no better. Tariffs, the main economic tool of the government since the time of John A. Macdonald, were of little use in a world where there was no trade to tax. Indeed, the Tory anglophile Bennett had actually *reduced* duties on British cars in 1932, hurting the Canadian industry even more. For his part, King oversaw significant tariff changes in 1936, but they did nothing to alleviate the underlying problems of the Depression, namely overcapacity and a paucity of purchasing power. Almost as bad as the lack of solutions was the fact that both leaders seemed so oblivious to the depths of despair to which average Canadians plummeted in the mid-1930s.

George Burt could have told both Bennett and King a thing or two about what was going on, at least for the ordinary Canadian working in the auto sector. Burt knew that the capitalist economic system, which had been responsible for the explosive growth of the auto industry, and which the automobile had done so much to advance, was in trouble. All across the country, protestors, politicians and ordinary people were demanding a new approach, creating new political parties and rethinking the way Canada worked. In places such as Burt's Oshawa, and Windsor, where auto workers faced the brunt of the Depression, people were determined to make changes. If the Liberals or Conservatives had no new ideas, there were other parties, new parties. The Canadian Commonwealth Federation and the Communist Party became very popular in this period and made strong inroads among auto workers.

One way to fight the Depression was for workers to get together,

Ford of Canada and Packard provided most of the ambulances that played a role in the Canadian and Allied war effort.

to bargain collectively and to force changes to the system. When Hugh Thompson, an organizer with the American-based United Auto Workers union, came to Oshawa in the spring of 1937, he had a willing ally in George Burt. In the United States, the UAW was having great success with its famous "sit-down strikes" and the time seemed right for action. Unionization was a necessary first step, and after a bitter eighteen-day strike, Local 222 gained a historic first contract with General Motors.

The GM contract was achieved against incredible odds: the union had to face down not just the company, but the fiery premier of Ontario, Mitch Hepburn. Hepburn called in the Mounties and even had his own personal brigade, the Sons of Mitches, ready to do battle against the union. In the end, Hepburn and GM had to concede, a stunning victory for Burt and Local 222. But Burt's enthusiasm must have been

tempered. Even with a contract, GM did not recognize the union, and all the auto companies remained vehemently opposed to the UAW. Moreover, even with the new security for Oshawa's auto workers, the Depression seemed to drag onward relentlessly.

It would take more than unionization to defeat the Depression. It would take a war. The impact of the Second World War upon the auto industry was dramatically different than that of the Great War. In the First World War, Canada's car industry had not been called upon by the government to deliver masses of war *matériel*. In fact, at a time when there were still a few Canadian auto firms operating, whatever motorized vehicles were procured by the Canadian military came from US-based or US-owned makers. Ironically, Thomas Russell, of Russell Motor Car fame, was appointed chief of procurement by Minister of Militia Sam Hughes. Russell purchased a few of his

Canada's auto industry became a northern arsenal of democracy during the Second World War. Building trucks at GM, circa 1943.

on in the conflict, were in stark contrast to that of his pacifist business associate, Henry Ford. Most importantly, during the First World War the vast majority of Canadian automakers continued to produce for public consumption and were not subject to government oversight.

The Second World War was entirely different for the Canadian auto industry. Adolf Hitler's fast, mobile blitzkrieg attacks in the fall of 1939 proved that mechanized vehicles were essential for any modern war effort. As the largest and most important manufacturing sector of the Canadian economy, the auto industry was capable of producing hundreds of thousands of such vehicles. As soon as the war broke out, the Canadian government began working with GM and Ford of Canada to provide vehicles for the military. For the first time, both companies needed to develop engineering departments to meet the specifications called for by the army. The result was the Canadian Military Pattern vehicle, of which more than four hundred thousand were eventually built for Canada and its allies.

The country's auto plants, however, did not become a true northern arsenal of democracy until the fall of France and the expulsion of the British army from Europe in 1940. Having lost all their equipment, the Brits ordered twenty-one thousand vehicles from the Canadians. This prompted the government to intercede directly

own company's cars (generating some conflict-of-interest investigations, which were eventually dropped) but did not reward Canadian companies. Russell did try to build a few armoured vehicles at his Toronto plant, but they were largely unsuccessful, and he converted to the production of artillery equipment in 1915, permanently ending vehicle production at the company.

Instead, firms such as Ford of Canada and Packard and White in the United States provided most of the trucks, ambulances, cars and armoured vehicles that played important roles in the Canadian and Allied effort. The biggest car of all during the war, the Model T, did play a prominent role on the battlefields of Europe, but not because the Canadian military was purchasing them. During the war, Ford of Canada exported more than forty thousand Model Ts directly to British forces, and Gordon McGregor's contributions to the war effort, especially early

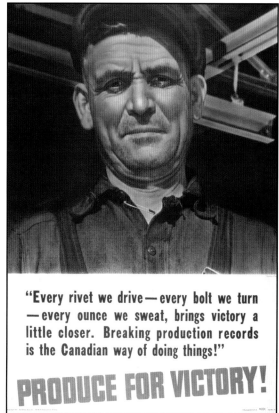

Wartime posters: Auto workers' and companies' efforts were reflected in the wartime propaganda that pushed production and patriotism.

to help Ford, GM and the other Canadian automakers meet the new production demands. Ottawa funded the factories at Windsor and Oshawa with millions of dollars for new facilities, tooling and equipment.

Military orders zoomed, and the unused capacity and slowdowns of the Depression were quickly forgotten. Along with military vehicles, Canadian car companies provided all kinds of *matériel* for the war effort, from anti-tank guns, to shells, to airplane parts. It was an astounding show of industrial might. With the demands of

war, passenger-car production slowed and was eventually stopped by 1942. With all material destined for the factories, rationing of gas, rubber tires and parts made car use rare during the war.

While GM, Ford and Chrysler boosted production and profitability, they also played upon their patriotism. With no civilian car production to advertise, they instead advertised their wartime efforts to Canadians in an effort not only to quell any criticisms of wartime profiteering, but also to remind consumers that once the war ended, their cars would be back on the market. The ads

Not just Rosie the Riveter: A Canadian Women's Army Corps (CWAC) service member pumping up the tires of a staff car, Ottawa, circa 1945.

showed that Canada had mobilized for the war and that the auto industry had been at the forefront of the most demanding endeavour in the country's history. The auto industry's products were with the Canadian army during the invasion of Italy, at the D-Day landings on Juno Beach, all through the liberation of Holland and in countless other engagements during the war. The vehicles and *matériel* built by the Canadian Big Three and the rest of the industry were indispensable for fighting the war and were an important part of the Allied victories around the world.

Orchestrating this massive effort with the auto companies was Minister of Munitions C.D. Howe. Howe, who was originally from the United States, was incredibly effective in marshalling the nation's resources toward the war effort. He reorganized industries, created new industries from practically nothing and focused Canada's manufacturing sector to maximum effect. Because Howe's reach over the economy was so widespread, he quickly got the nickname Minister of Everything. By the end of the war, Howe and the Canadian auto industry had overseen the production of more than eight hundred thousand military vehicles.

Obviously, this booming war production required a huge labour force. In 1938, with the Depression still going, nearly one in six Canadians was unemployed. By 1942, that number had dropped to less than 2 percent, and nearly two million Canadians were in war-related jobs, along with the one million who were in the army. It was, essentially, full employment for the first time in the country's history. In fact, by 1942, there was a worker shortage, and a government permit was required for a worker to switch jobs, especially in the highly sensitive auto industry.

If the quintessential image of the home front in the Second World War remains Rosie the Riveter, it is probably because she was working in a converted auto plant, right alongside men such as Burt. With the labour shortage, 373,000 women joined the manufacturing sector during the war, thousands of them at auto plants across the country. These workers became a backbone of the war effort and signalled a departure from women's traditional roles in society. The war liberated thousands of women to work but only to a degree — their jobs were circumscribed by ideas of what was considered "womanly," and therefore suitable, work; they were paid less, and governments and employers viewed their playing these new roles as just a temporary measure.

General View Of Car Munitions (Tanks) Shop, Angus Shop, Montreal, *by Frederick Bourchier Taylor (1906-1987). This painting reflected the intensity and scale of the wartime production. After the war, Canada's factories would be converted again to produce hundreds of thousands of cars.*

With so many Canadians in the factories building essential *matériel* for the wartime effort, it seemed to be the perfect time to advance worker rights, particularly in the auto sector. George Burt understood early on that labour peace was necessary during a time of war in order to ensure that industries were running to their full capacity. But neither the auto companies nor the government had made it easy on workers. Burt's own UAW Local 222 at Oshawa had still not been recognized by GM, while Ford remained adamantly opposed to the union. For its part, Ottawa froze wages in the manufacturing industries to prevent inflation. Wage levels, moreover, were kept at Depression levels, which caused hardship for workers.

At the start of the war, Burt had been elected leader of the Canadian side of the UAW. He recognized that for many workers, this was the perfect time to strike in order to gain recognition and to challenge wage freezes. Burt led a series of strikes at auto plants across southern Ontario, where the industry was concentrated. He was charged with interfering with war production for leading a picket at Chrysler's Windsor plant in 1940. Yet Burt and his fellows in the auto sector were not the only workers striking for better pay and working conditions and union recognition. In war-sensitive industries, such as coal and steel, there were major strikes from 1941 to 1943. Obviously, this caused massive disruption for the war effort. In 1943, strike days by Canadian workers added up to more than one million. Labour was on the march as it had not been since the days of the Winnipeg General Strike.

Faced with these difficulties, and feeling the pressure of an upcoming election campaign, the federal Liberal government finally passed the National War Labour Order, or PC 1003, in 1944. This law guaranteed all workers in all industries the right to vote on a union and introduced compulsory collective bargaining on the national level. As a result, most unions agreed to forgo strikes for the duration of the war; in 1944, strike days were half of what they had been the year before. PC 1003 was really the Magna Carta of the labour movement in Canada, and it gave unions a strong starting point for recognition and rights. Unionization grew tremendously in Canada after that. In 1939, there were about three hundred and fifty thousand unionized workers in Canada. By 1945, that number had increased to more than seven hundred thousand.

The auto sector had led the way in this victory for union rights in Canada. In 1942, Ford of Canada had reluctantly agreed to grant their workers the right to vote on the union. The federal government had pressured the company to do so after Burt and the workers at Ford had threatened to disrupt the production of vital military parts. When the vote was held, Ford workers solidly endorsed Burt's UAW.

It was the same story at auto plants across the country: by 1942, Chrysler workers had voted for the union overwhelmingly, as had dozens of other small parts makers, aircraft makers and other manufacturers. Nonetheless, like the UAW's victory at GM in 1937, this was only a partial success. Ford still refused to recognize the UAW as the sole representative of the workers and did not accept the idea of a "check off" — that union dues be automatically deducted from Ford pay slips.

The end of the war brought a temporary joyous interlude in the fight for union recognition. In May and August of 1945, Canadians across the country celebrated the victories in Europe and the Pacific. Revellers swarmed city streets, danced, kissed, drove and drank to the Canadian and Allied victories. After six long years of war, all Canadians could take pride in the achievements of the fighting forces abroad and the millions of workers on the home front.

In the fall of 1945, George Burt and his allies again took up their own fight. This time, the target was Ford's massive operations in Windsor, which employed fourteen thousand workers.

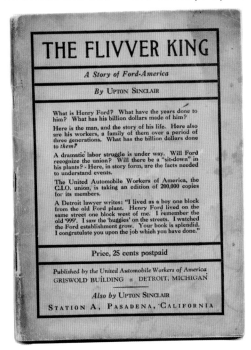

THE FLIVVER KING

A Story of Ford-America

By UPTON SINCLAIR

What is Henry Ford? What have the years done to him? What has his billion dollars made of him?

Here is the man, and the story of his life. Here also are his workers, a family of them over a period of three generations. What has the billion dollars done to *them*?

A dramatic labor struggle is under way. Will Ford recognize the union? Will there be a "sit-down" in his plants? - Here, in story form, are the facts needed to understand events.

The United Automobile Workers of America, the C.I.O. union, is taking an edition of 200,000 copies for its members.

A Detroit lawyer writes: "I lived as a boy one block from the old Ford plant. Henry Ford lived on the same street one block west of me. I remember the old '999'. I saw the 'buggies' on the streets. I watched the Ford establishment grow. Your book is splendid. I congratulate you upon the job which you have done."

Price, 25 cents postpaid

Published by the United Automobile Workers of America
GRISWOLD BUILDING :: DETROIT, MICHIGAN

Also by UPTON SINCLAIR
STATION A, PASADENA, CALIFORNIA

Henry Ford's relationship with his employees, like so many other aspects of the man, was contradictory. After announcing his Five Dollar Day in 1914, Henry Ford had been hailed as a champion of the working man. Thousands of men had poured into Detroit and Windsor to work for Ford Motor, and the company had basked in the glow of praise from average Canadians and Americans.

But the Ford story also had a dark side. Ford expected his employees not just to work in a particular manner, but to live a particular way as well. He established a Sociological Department, which attempted to control every aspect of his workers' lives outside of the factory gates, just as "scientific management" controlled every motion on the assembly line. Ford's sociological agents would come into an employee's home to see if the house was being kept clean, or keep an eye on Windsor's bars to make sure Mr. Ford's workers were not wasting their earnings on drink.

More dangerously, Ford was dead-set against unions and employed a small army of vicious "security" men to spy on, intimidate and sometimes physically threaten workers, particularly those who were interested in a union. As Ford of Canada's operations were a stone's throw directly across the river from Ford's giant American plant, the Canadian firm never strayed far from its progenitor's practices. The publication of *The Flivver King*, a popular 1937 working-class novel about Ford and his brutal approach, exposed some of the less-honourable tendencies of Ford, but did not change the man or his company's ideas about unions, either in the United States or Canada.

Although Ford had accepted a first union contract in 1942, the UAW still had not achieved recognition and security for its membership.

Left: The Flivver King, *Upton Sinclair's muckraking exposé about labour practices at Ford, helped to galvanize workers in the auto industry. Above: The car as a tool in the battle for automotive labour rights: using autos to blockade Ford's Windsor facility, 1945.*

Ford workers were determined to set the pattern for the rest of the industry and began a massive strike. Soon, they were joined in a sympathy strike by more than five thousand workers at Chrysler and other parts plants in Windsor. Five weeks into the strike, with the company determined to defeat the workers by any means necessary, union leaders decided to block company security guards from entry to the Ford plant. With this escalation in the battle, it seemed likely that the Mounties would be called in to break the strike by force.

Then something extraordinary happened. The Ford strikers and their allies dramatically utilized an unlikely new tool in their battle against the company: the car itself. Taking a page out of their American counterparts' book, Ford workers used their cars to blockade the plant and all the roads leading to the Ford of Canada factories. Thousands of cars clogged the roads, the overpasses, the side streets and practically every nook and cranny of the area around Ford in Windsor. The sea of cars and people not only prevented the company or the Mounties from breaking the strike, but it also proved to Ford that the fight to keep the union out was a lost cause. Burt and his co-workers and colleagues won the day.

As a result of the Ford strike, the two sides agreed that Judge Ivan Rand be appointed to arbitrate between the union and the company. Rand ruled that Ford was obliged to include a union dues check-off, which meant recognition of the union. It also meant that all workers at Ford would be required to pay their dues, even if they did not wish to be represented by the UAW. It was an important step for auto workers in the union movement in Canada, and the Rand Formula was soon standard for contracts across the industry, even, finally, at General Motors in Oshawa.

The Ford victory and the Rand Formula symbolized a new status for the UAW and for unions in general in Canada. The end of the war had elicited the concern that labour unrest would return, as it had following the end of the First World War, most notably at Winnipeg. But the Rand Formula, and the ability of the UAW to bargain for better wages and job security (both in the United States and in Canada), meant that economic prosperity spread to blue-collar, working-class families. This was a significant moment for the industry and the country, as the looming post-war demographic and economic boom provided an opportunity for the car to transform Canada. The new status of the UAW provided Canadian auto workers with the highest standard of living for workers in the country's history *and* gave those same workers the purchasing power to buy cars — cars that would again remake the Canadian landscape.

The return to civilian production after 1945 represented a new, more powerful auto industry, yet one that had been changed fundamentally. The war had turned Canada's Big Three into the largest manufacturing concerns the country had ever seen, employing thousands of people and building hundreds of thousands of cars. Unions now played a central role in the life of the industry and garnered the loyalty of thousands of company employees. Because of the work of George Burt and his colleagues, a Ford man was no longer just a Ford man — he was a UAW man too. The hard-won financial gains of workers in the bitter labour campaigns of the 1930s and 1940s meant that a new middle class was emerging in Canada, one that would spread its wealth and status across the nation through its symbol, the automobile. After two decades of uncertainty, of Depression and war, the car was back, and its reign would be glorious.

FOUR

King Car: The Automobile's Golden Age

The golden age of the car in Canada coincided with the greatest and most prolonged boom in North American history. The automobile was the iconic symbol of this generational shift in Canadian life and personified the dazzling potential of what many saw as the height of modernity. The automobile emblems of the era — from the 1953 Corvette, to the tail fins of the 1950s Cadillacs, to the 1965 Mustang — were more than just steel and chrome. They represented a new industrial might, a new ethos of consumption and a new understanding by Canadians of their dependency on and identification with cars.

The great post-war boom that followed the Second World War cemented the car's place at the centre of Canadian life. Between 1941 and 1962, Canada's population increased from 11.5 million to 18.5 million, an incredible 60 percent. Amazingly, the boom in cars outpaced that of the population. In the years after the war, Canadians bought cars on an unprecedented scale. In 1941, just more than one-third of Canadian households owned a car. By 1971, it was more than four-fifths. Put another way, between 1945 and 1973, the Canadian population increased 83 percent, yet the number of cars increased an astounding 577 percent.

The auto industry itself was a main cause of this incredible growth and prosperity. The war had meant that virtually all consumer products, including cars, were restricted due to the necessities of wartime output. There had been no

The Chevy Bel Air epitomized the style and consumerism of the 1950s cars.

Ford's new Oakville plant, opened in 1954, reflected the amazing growth and strength of the postwar auto industry in Canada.

the fortunes of the automobile industry.

The great car-induced boom was sparked by more than just Canadian post-war consumer demand. Although the Canadian industry still lay largely behind the nineteenth-century protectionist wall that had helped to create the sector, it benefited from the fact that most of the other auto-producing nations, especially England, Germany and Italy, lay in ruins. Taking advantage of this competitive advantage, between 1946 and 1955, Canadian carmakers exported nearly 175,000 autos to Europe and parts of the Commonwealth. Production for the home market, boosted by exports, helped to create a vibrant, expanding industry. By the end of the 1950s, the auto sector had become the uncontested champion of a new, industrial Canada.

production of civilian cars at all since 1942. In the post-war period, pent-up demand led to an automotive surge, and as veterans returned and suburbs were built, Canadians hurried to their local dealers for the latest model vehicles.

By the late 1940s, the Canadian auto industry was booming again as it had been in the 1920s. Production of vehicles increased from 92,000 to 375,000 between 1946 and 1954, and employment in the industry increased as well, from 22,000 to 29,000. The Canadian auto industry was back — with a bang. Ford opened a new headquarters and plant in Oakville in 1954, and GM and Chrysler both added to their production. By the 1960s, these three subsidiary companies were among Canada's largest and most profitable. GM was the country's largest private employer, and Ford and Chrysler dominated whole cities' economies. As the country settled back into civilian life, the economy became increasingly tied to

Labour peace helped fuel this auto-driven prosperity. The bitter unionization battles of the 1930s and 1940s gave way to a much more co-operative relationship between the United Auto Workers (UAW) and the Big Three. The 1950 "Treaty of Detroit" between the union and the companies was pivotal in ensuring continued production and shared prosperity. In return for increased wages and job security, the UAW offered the car companies production certainty and the promise to police their own workers. Following upon the American pattern, Canadian auto workers also gained from this consensus and prosperity in the sector, which tremendously boosted the growth of Canada's middle class.

George Burt's tenure reflected this accommodation: he remained head of the Canadian UAW until 1968. The high wages Burt helped to negotiate in the auto industry set the standard for workers, and spilled into other sectors of the economy giving Canadians the ability to purchase the millions of cars churned out by Windsor, Oshawa, Oakville and Detroit.

And what cars they were. Like their American cousins, Canadians revelled in the glory of Detroit's fabulous automotive fashions. While the Canadian Big Three did not design any of the cars, they basked in the artistic flair of their parent companies' emphasis upon style and the annual model change. These annual model changes, implemented by Alfred Sloan at GM in the 1920s, were the rage of the industry by the 1950s, and resulted in a host of new vehicles to choose from every year. Canadians clamoured for Detroit's designs and enthusiastically assumed the consumer posture that prevailed in the period, eagerly anticipating the new models and buying cars as often as they could. American cars had created a Canadian "community of consumption."

By the mid-1950s, American cars had become the global standard and represented the height of consumer desire. Long, brightly coloured cars with big engines, huge tail fins and luxurious interiors rolled off the assembly lines in a dizzy-

Chrome, steel, tail fins, lights, bumpers, big engines and whitewalls in a dizzying variety of styles and models rolled off the assembly lines in Detroit, Windsor, Oshawa and Oakville in the 1950s.

ing variety and number of styles and models. Shiny dashboards, vibrantly colourful leather seats, contoured windows and chrome bumpers and grilles became standard features of 1950s models. Of course, in a few years many would complain in car magazines and consumer reports that car designers had gone overboard in an attempt to "out-fin" one another. Author John Keats's 1958 *Insolent Chariots* summed up the criticism of the post-war car: the 1950s driver "crawls into an illuminated rolling cave and then reclines on a sort of couch, there to push

American auto-Zeitgeist a little later, and at times with a little less vigour, but there was no question that they easily saw themselves reflected in the values that Detroit's shiny, curvy cars of the 1950s came to symbolize. If the suburban home, the white picket fence and the ubiquitous car in the driveway represented the American dream, it represented the Canadian dream, too.

The perfect woman's car: In the Golden Age of cars, traditional notions of male and female roles and family dominated.

Foremost for Americans (and Canadians, in fact) in the post-war period was the notion of family. One significant difference with the 1920s boom was that this time, Canadians were "homeward bound." The end of the war, the return of veterans, the fears of the Cold War and (most importantly) the seemingly overwhelming presence of children all created an atmosphere wherein "traditional" notions of family prevailed. Marriage rates increased, and, astonishingly, there were no less than 400,000 babies born in Canada annually between 1952 and 1966. The baby boom generation — wealthy, confident and immense in numbers — had a distinctive relationship with cars, one that would profoundly influence societal trends for decades to come, on both sides of the border.

buttons and idly wonder what might lie in front of the glittering hood, while the sun burns into the eyes through the slanted windshield that is strangely overhead." But for many others and most consumers, the cars of the post-war period were the zenith of American ingenuity, innovation and style.

The cars themselves represented something more than American style: they represented American values as well. This new post-war automobile culture that Canadians adopted in the late 1940s and 1950s was prosperous, consumerist and suburban. Yet it also reflected traditional notions of the family, male and female roles, class and ethnicity. Canadians may have embraced this

The baby boom was first felt in the emergence of the "family" car, a designation that had not really been part of the automotive marketing vocabulary before the war. The "nuclear family," sheltered together in their home and their car in the atomic age, was a defining image of the 1950s. Station wagons and large, roomy sedans with gigantic trunks were seen as a necessity for

Suburban dreams in a nuclear age: The 1953 Ford Crestline Convertible in the perfect driveway.

the Canadian family in a child-centred world. The "family car" became the staple of post-war Canadian identity and a central image in so many photos of the suburban landscape.

This family-oriented ethos affected women tremendously. Women still drove, and drove in greater numbers than ever before. But their roles were far more circumscribed than the roles of women in the Roaring Twenties or during the war. Women behind the wheel in the 1950s were not devil-may-care "flappers" flashing their newly won freedom or workers heading off to the munitions factory, but homemakers running domestic errands and mothers chauffeuring children. Societal pressures were placed upon women to stay at home and be mothers, and though many women still worked outside the home, it was considered unseemly by many and discouraged. Thus, even in a period of prosperity and auto freedom, the 1950s limited women's role to mother and wife. Many women revelled in this role and enjoyed the renewed emphasis on family; many others chafed under the constraints. In an era of conservative values, trends and politics, the car-dependent suburb became a trap for many women.

At the same time, the car also influenced ideas of masculinity. From the first construction and use of cars by men, the automobile had been connected with what it meant to be a man,

A 1965 Mustang: The "muscle car" personified masculinity and confidence for many baby-boomer Canadian men.

interpreted in images on film, in advertising and in the news. Being "behind the wheel" or "in the driver's seat" was to be in command. Driver safety courses and advertising stressed that a good driver was also a good man, and a successful man. New categories of "sports cars," "muscle cars," and "pony cars" were all marketed to men in ads playing on notions of toughness and masculinity, and the "manliness" of many types of vehicles quickly became one of the distinguishing traits of linking cars and traditional male roles. Cars with names such as Thunderbird, Corvette and Mustang reflected the muscular, confident American and, by extension, Canadian man.

Age, too, and the generational gap quickly became defined and redefined by the car. With the proliferation of automobiles in Canadian families, especially the growing Canadian middle-class families, cars became an essential part of many children's formative years and a touchstone along the passage into young adulthood. The widespread use of cars by "teenagers" — from the first access to a car, to licensing and the ability to drive, to buying one's own "first car" — were signposts on the road to adulthood.

And from being able to get off the farm, to the quaint notion of dating Happy Days–style in the 1950s, to the sexual liberation of the 1960s, the

car became a vehicle with which to challenge authority and escape watchful eyes. From "cruising" to "parking" to "drive-ins," the car created new venues for romantic interludes and broke down the boundaries of sexual constraint. The new music that defined teenagers, rock 'n' roll, was infused with the freedom of the car, and music from Elvis to the Beach Boys pulsated with the beat of the car's rhythm. More than any other aspect, liberation defined the baby boom generation, and the car provided that liberation and sense of self-confidence in the 1950s and 1960s.

Some cars came to define youthful exuberance. In the 1950s, teenaged Canadians followed their cool American cousins by buying Chevy Bel Airs and cruising California-style (the car was produced in Canada until 1981). In the 1960s, young Canadians bought thousands of inexpensive, quirky Volkswagen Beetles. On one level, these cars, built by Germans ("What would your father think?!"), represented a challenge to their parents and to the Big Three car-buying establishment. Later in the decade, young Canadians bought powerful Camaros or Mustangs, emulating screen heroes such as Steve McQueen. In the golden age, cars were the glamorous icons of youth and possibility, and their owners basked in their glorious reflection.

Social status and ethnic background was a part of this sense of self too. In the 1920s, the automobile had been a central agent in the creation of both modern consumerism and of notions of class. Alfred Sloan's "ladder" of cars, from the "common man" Chevy to the exclusive Cadillac, returned with a vengeance after the war. Canadians of all social and ethnic backgrounds aspired to the ideal of prosperity and upward

The suburbs spread rapidly in this prosperous, booming period, helped along by the car. Edmonton, 1953.

social mobility exemplified by autos and their status-enhancing power. The car became an outward sign of success and acceptance, that one fit in or belonged. Cars were affordable enough that most Canadians, new immigrants and the long established alike, could fulfill the (North) American dream of buying a car and sharing in the pride of car ownership.

While family, gender, age and class were being changed in the golden age of cars, nowhere was the impact of American ideals more obvious than in the car-centric "suburbia" in the post–Second World War period. American developments such as New York's Levittown, built between 1947 and 1951, pioneered the new type of living. Thousands of families (and their cars) moved to corporate, planned suburbs just like Levittown all over the United States in the late 1940s and early 1950s, drawn by the dream of family space, home ownership, convenience, newness and safety. In the post-war period, suburbia was, for many, the closest thing to utopia imaginable.

Canadians were not far behind in their affection for the new suburbs. From the edge of Vancouver, to the booming subdivisions of Toronto, to the South Shore of Montreal, planned communities became the epitome of "modern" Canada. The garage, the driveway, the cul-de-sac became common parlance, impressing themselves onto our mental and physical landscapes with a sense of permanence. The new suburbs were also sometimes generic and homogeneous. This was not surprising: government mortgage and veterans' benefits policies, and housing and

With its sprawling parking lots, the postwar mall became the ultimate car-oriented consumer space. Hamilton, 1959.

building codes, all facilitated the growth of these sprawling developments. In the 1950s, however, they were praised as the height of sophisticated, civilized living. To this day, the suburban ideal dominates many Canadians' views of what it means to be "successful" and to be in a proper "family home" in the twenty-first century.

The sameness of the suburbs, with their endless grid of roadways and rows of houses, driveways and garages, fit perfectly with the values of the period. Family, conformity and consumerism, which all reflected the Cold-War conservatism of the period, all melded together to produce a similarity of space and place across the country. Don Mills, the first post-war suburb of Toronto, opened in 1953 as a single, corporate development. It became the prototype of subsequent planned Canadian suburbs, wherein all the commercial aspects, schools and phases of houses were built by a single developer. It was

also a turning point in the design of neighbourhoods in that it utilized for the first time curvy streets instead of a grid pattern.

Other Canadian cities followed this model, and soon enough, Don Mills–like suburbs were being built in places as diverse as Calgary, Montreal, Ottawa and Winnipeg. Families flowed to these suburban destinations, assured that their cars would provide them with an easy, comfortable connection to the outside world.

Along with the suburbs came the next generation of car infrastructure. The 1920s had seen a vast buildup of gas stations, mechanics, car dealerships and a host of other auto-related changes to the landscape. But the golden age pushed the car's impact upon the landscape to a breathtaking level. Roadside culture such as drive-ins, drive-thru restaurants, parking lots and new shopping malls spread rapidly in the prosperous 1950s and 1960s.

Indoor shopping malls, one of the greatest symbols of the car-oriented culture of the period, sprouted up across the country and were designed for automobiles almost as much as they were for people. Gigantic parking lots encircled these privately owned and operated consumer palaces, which were largely inaccessible without a car. For Canadians, these new, covered and climate-controlled structures offered a respite from the elements, be it the cold and snow of the winter or the sweltering heat of the summer.

Positioned strategically near highways and suburbs, malls became the new meeting places of post-war Canada, refashioning shopping, living and the landscape between suburb and city. By the end of the 1950s, virtually every Canadian city had a mall, and the notion of walking or taking transit "downtown" to some storefront shopping district seemed quaint and outmoded. In 1950, the Park City Mall in West Vancouver became the first covered mall in Canada. Polo Park Mall in Winnipeg opened on the outskirts of the city in 1959. In Toronto, Yorkdale Mall was built beside Highway 401 in 1964. By the 1960s, King Car had displaced the very public mingling of citizen and street with the private interaction of consumer, car and mall.

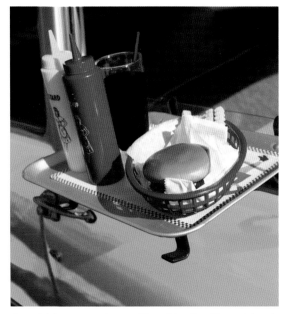

Roadside car culture, like this Car-Hop drive-in restaurant in Brantford, Ontario, grew almost as quickly as the postwar Canadian population. Below: A clip-on tray reflected Canadians' growing connection between driving and eating.

But the mall was just one of the most visible signs of a world inundated with cars. Roadside culture became pervasive during the golden age.

The highways and byways of the postwar period became the arteries of the nation, even more than the rails of a previous century. Paving Highway 401 in Toronto, near Avenue Road, 1958.

Indeed, the notion of a "golden mile" became commonplace in Canada — a strip of auto-oriented consumerism that was present in virtually every town or city. Parking lots became the defining feature of these car-friendly, pedestrian-averse spaces, which contained stores selling everything from shoes to groceries, as well as banks, offices and a host of other services and amenities, all most easily accessed by car.

Restaurants in particular were a new, always-present feature of the revitalized Canadian carscape. From humble beginnings, franchises and chains quickly spread across the country. Burger joints, drive-thrus, carhops, truck stops and diners became as familiar and generic a sight on

Canadian highways and streets as gas stations and street signs. Canadians quickly became accustomed to the notion that the car was inexorably connected to eating (indeed, many Canadians liked the notion of eating in cars too).

The rapid spread of car-oriented restaurants was a testament to this notion. Although Vancouver's White Spot had started as a drive-thru operation in the 1920s, the company quickly spread all across the West in the 1940s and 1950s. Back east, Harvey's started in Richmond Hill in 1959, Mr. Donut in Toronto in 1961 and Tim Hortons in Hamilton in 1962. McDonald's, the omnipresent American franchise, did not actually enter Canada until 1967,

Gas stations became an indispensable and ubiquitous element of the roadside car culture that gripped the Canadian landscape during motordom's Golden Age.

opening their first restaurant in Richmond, BC. Burger King made their own Canadian appearance, fittingly, in Windsor, in 1969.

By this time, roadside culture permeated the Canadian landscape. Motels, hotels, churches, bowling alleys, restaurants, gas stations, parking garages and innumerable signs of all types and formats cluttered streets to the point of distraction. Some Canadians decried this "visual pollution" and launched campaigns to "stop the car," or at least slow its impact upon older commercial and residential areas, especially in smaller towns and in heritage districts. But the relentless expansion of the car-oriented sprawl continued largely unimpeded. By the 1960s, Canadians could scarcely imagine a world in which cars and roadside culture had not always been a factor in their daily lives.

The growth of suburbs and roadside culture was fed by the car, but the car itself needed roads to spread. The post-war golden age of the car was also a golden age of road and highway building. In 1949, the federal and provincial governments struck a deal to finish the Trans-Canada

The holiday getaway: Heading north to cottage country on Highway 400, Dominion Day weekend, July 1967.

Highway, a massive project that was finally completed in 1962, fifty years after Jack Haney and Thomas Wilby had embarked upon their treacherous cross-Canada road trip. The Trans-Canada, whose arduous completion was akin to the construction of the Canadian Pacific Railway, became a symbol of the new age of cars.

Along with the "national road," provinces and towns built their own highways and roads. In 1939, altogether, municipalities in Canada spent $18.7 million on roads. By 1953, governments were spending $100 million a year on road construction. As with so many other aspects of the car's influence, Canadian governments were also inspired by the massive highway-building projects in the United States, which created a national system criss-crossing America in the 1950s.

In Canada, new "freeways" sprouted: the Crowsnest Highway was opened in British Columbia in 1949. The Canso Causeway was built in 1955, allowing travel by road between Cape Breton and mainland Nova Scotia. Highway construction in Quebec boomed in the 1960s, as the province used road building as another aspect of its state-building Quiet Revolution policies and geared up for the Expo

Space for cars became as important as space for people, especially at tourist sites. Parking to see Niagara Falls, 1959.

'67 festivities. The 401 was completed in 1961 linking Ontario to Quebec in the east and of course Windsor and the United States in the southwest. The Gardiner Expressway (1954) and the Don Valley Parkway (1961) burrowed into and across downtown Toronto, and highways sprouted north to cottage country. Canadians could now speed all across their country in the privacy and comfort of their automobiles.

All of this massive road construction led to a renewed boom in travel and tourism. In British Columbia, governments and business promoted tourism that emphasized the province's rugged landscape and its "Britishness" as a way to draw motor travellers west and north from the United States. In Quebec, promoters emphasized the province's cultural distinctiveness and its fishing and hunting destinations, now easily accessible by car. Ontario's traditional cottage destinations and resort and beach towns, from Muskoka to Wasaga to the Kawarthas, experienced a new influx of travellers.

By the mid-1950s, it seemed that every Canadian family had undertaken some sort of "road trip" vacation. From coast to coast, people hopped in their cars and headed out across their

Streetcars, once the primary mode of travel for city-dwellers, became increasingly endangered as cities shifted their focus to accommodating the massive increase in cars.

great country — not on the rails of the CPR or the CNR, but on the new ties that bound Canada together, its roads. The completion of the Trans-Canada and various other highways gave Canadians a new sense of freedom within their own country and a new sense of its opportunities.

Of course, notwithstanding all of its positive aspects, the period was not always golden. As in the 1920s, car accidents soared with the boom in automobile usage. By the mid-1960s, nearly 5,000 Canadians a year were being killed on the roads, a carnage that automakers and governments largely blamed upon human error. In response, they focused upon driver education, which stressed the "manliness" of the safe operator. Safety features such as seat belts, shatter-proof glass and better bumpers and less

powerful automobiles could have cut the number of road casualties, but this type of regulation and awareness was still emerging and would not become central to Canadians' car concerns until the end of the 1960s.

Thousands of these fatalities were of pedestrians, as cars and people continued to battle over who owned the streets in the cities and suburbs of the nation. In the 1930s and 1940s, the Depression and war had momentarily slowed motordom's ascendance over the streetscape. With scarcity, rationing and conservation governing Canadians' driving behaviour, transit boomed in this period. The street railways flourished, and cars, while still in use, were forced to share the street with other modes of traffic.

The golden age marked the death knell for this traffic co-existence. In the late 1940s and 1950s, cities and towns gave themselves over almost entirely to the automobile. The electric street railways, which had been a feature of Canadian cities since the nineteenth century, were no match for the "modernity" of the car. With millions of Canadians purchasing cars, moving to suburbs and driving on highways, the car's dominion over the surface thoroughfares of the nation was seemingly irresistible. City planners and politicians, more concerned with road building for cars and buses, killed off their public streetcars in favour of private cars.

All across the country, municipalities tore up their tracks to make way for the car. Vancouver ended its electric streetcar service in 1947; Victoria, in 1948; St. John's and Halifax, in 1949. Saskatoon and Edmonton in 1951; and Montreal and Ottawa in 1959. Smaller cities, such as St. Catharines and Sudbury in Ontario and Nelson in British Columbia, also discontinued their streetcar services.

More than any other event, the decimation of the electric street railways symbolized the victory of King Car over the Canadian landscape and its

The importance of streetcars could be seen in the symbolic flipping of one during the 1919 Winnipeg General Strike. By the 1950s, Winnipeggers indicated their preference for their cars by abolishing streetcars entirely from their streets.

consequences. Winnipeg provides perhaps the best example of the impact of the car. As the greatest Canadian boomtown of the nineteenth-century wheat economy, Winnipeg had experienced an incredibly fast growth between the 1880s and the 1920s. Its first electric street railway commenced service in 1891, and by the time of the Winnipeg General Strike in 1919, the city's system was extensive. So central was the streetcar to the city's civic life that during the strike, the flipping of the streetcars was a political act heavy with symbolism. Usage along busy main routes, such as Portage Avenue, made the Winnipeg system one of the most heavily used in the country.

In the 1950s, Winnipeg tore up its streetcar tracks, and the last streetcar made its final run in 1955. In the 1960s and the 1970s, the city redeveloped its downtown and main intersection of Portage and Main almost entirely to meet the needs of cars. With the end of streetcars, the vibrant urban life that had characterized Winnipeg slowly eroded; as the city's suburbs flourished, cars became the preferred mode of transportation, and fewer and fewer people came downtown. When they did come downtown, the cityscape was now marked by parking lots and parking garages, while storefront shopping had quietly and slowly disappeared. Many Canadians welcomed the end of streetcars as

Endangered coexistence: By the 1960s, Toronto was the only major Canadian city that retained its streetcar system. Montreal's, pictured here in 1943, would be ripped up in 1959.

a sign of progress, but others mourned their disappearance.

The story of Winnipeg's surrender to the convenience and status of the car is but one tale of the consequences of motordom's victory. Other consequences would become much more apparent in the years after Canada celebrated its centennial in 1967. By then, Canadians were beginning to realize that King Car was no benevolent monarch, and that the problems inherent in the automobile's reign could sometimes outweigh the benefits that it bestowed. The car's relentless revolution, only temporarily stalled by the Depression and the war, reached the height of its power in the period between 1946 and 1973. This was true, too, of the auto industry itself: the golden age of building cars would soon become much more complicated, largely because of forces outside of Canadians' control. In 1973, Canadians, wedded to their cars, would face another kind of revolution. This revolution would come in the form of a shock that rippled across the globe and struck at the very lifeblood of the car: oil.

FIVE

Driving into the World, From Oil Crisis to Today

The cataclysmic oil shock in October 1973 did not end the golden age of the car in Canada. When the Organization of the Petroleum Exporting Countries (OPEC) began their oil embargo against the West in response to the Arab-Israeli Yom Kippur War, it struck at the heart of the auto industry, North America's and Europe's most important economic engines. The embargo sent shock waves around the world, particularly in the United States. The effect was not so traumatic in Canada, which was less dependent upon imported oil at the time.

Canadians, however, were well aware of the impact of the embargo upon their southern neighbours. One only had to tune in to the nightly newscasts to see the images of gas station lineups and hear the bewilderment of ordinary Americans, who felt as though their birthright — to drive as much as they wanted to, in cars as big as they wanted them to be — had been unfairly, suddenly ripped from them.

No, the oil shock did not mean the end of car production or the end of Canadians' love affair with the car. But there was no doubt that the prosperous and freewheeling golden age of the car gave way to a much different landscape after the 1960s. This new landscape reflected a radical departure for the car and its industry. Yet the long-standing questions about Canada's direction as a nation owing much of its modern form to motordom continued.

An image for a new age of oil and uncertainty: Filling up in Calgary, 1971.

The gas shortages and new mileage requirements prompted some to try to make light of the situation: A joke image mocks fuel economy demands, 1976.

Since the car's first dusty, loud appearance in the late nineteenth century, the auto and its industry had represented more than just the tremendous changes to place, space and people. It represented something of a proxy for the battle over the very soul of Canada. Nationalism, continentalism and globalization were three strains that had, since the time of Sir Wilfrid Laurier, tugged at Canada and its auto industry in three very different ways.

After all, the nationalism of John A. Macdonald's National Policy of tariffs had initially created the branch-plant existence of the Canadian industry in the early part of the century, as Gordon McGregor, Sam McLaughlin and all the other auto pioneers would surely have attested to. McGregor had pushed the Canadianness of his cars, as had McLaughlin, and both Ford and GM had used patriotism before, during, and after the Second World War. Nationalism was a key factor in building, buying and selling cars.

But McGregor and McLaughlin would also have recognized, as did many Canadians, that although it was an impulse to protect Canadian industry that led John A. to build his tariff wall, the resulting edifice was squarely continental in its implications. Ford of Canada, and most of the Canadian industry, existed and flourished in the

The British Mini became a popular car in Canada in the postwar period. In the twenty-first century the "new" Mini, pictured here, was popular again.

early age of the car because of its continental ties. Canadians had benefited immensely by their proximity to the United States, from the democratizing impact of Henry Ford's mass-market desires, to the spread of new technologies and styles, to the American suburban ideals that seeped across the border.

The Canadian industry had, even from its very beginnings, also been connected to a global vision of the automobile. Canadians had gained their inspiration for the automobile from international examples, and the booms of the 1920s and 1950s had been in no small part because of the Canadian industry's huge exports to distant global markets. They had benefited, too, from a global outlook when it came to buying cars: Canadians bought VW Bugs, British Minis and early Toyotas in increasing numbers, even at the height of Detroit's golden age dominance.

These strains — nationalism, continentalism and globalization — shaped Canadians' connection to the automobile even more profoundly by the mid-1960s. At this point, the Canadian auto industry was the most important sector in the economy, accounting for the greatest amount of exports and imports and the most jobs. Nonetheless, it faced a number of problems. A small market, factories that were not up to the stylistic and technical demands of the cars of the golden age, and the difficulties of keeping pace with the incessant annual model change all threatened the industry. In order to maintain the auto industry's health, in 1965 Canadian Prime Minister Lester Pearson negotiated a new agreement with American President Lyndon Johnson that governed the two countries' trade in autos.

The agreement, a mix of nationalistic protectionism and continentalist free trade, integrated Canada's auto industry into that of the United States, forever eradicating John A.'s tariff wall for autos. Canada's branch-plant industry became a part of the United States, for all intents and purposes, allowing Canadian assemblers and parts makers to sell to the United States and their parent companies unimpeded. Able to build for the whole North American market, Canada's Big Three car plants were rationalized and updated.

Safety scares: In the 1960s and 1970s car safety became a major concern for people and their governments. Left, an early child-safety seat. Right, the Chevy Corvair, made famous by safety advocate Ralph Nader.

The Auto Pact sparked a boom in the industry in the late 1960s and early 1970s, as annual Canadian production more than doubled to over one million cars a year and employment zoomed from 30,000 to more than 50,000. Exports of finished cars to the United States became the staple of the industry, with more than 80 percent of production heading south. By the time of the 1973 oil shock, the Canadian industry was one of the most productive and successful in the world.

The 1973 embargo broke the run of post-war success for the automobile in Canada and ushered in a series of severe challenges for the car and its industry in the 1970s. Even before the Yom Kippur War, the American government had already begun to regulate the safety of automobiles after some tragic incidents had pointed to the need for better standards on cars. In 1966, consumer advocate Ralph Nader's dramatic testimony in front of the US Congress about how General Motors' cars (particularly the Chevy Corvair) were "unsafe at any speed" and the revelations that the company had spied on him shocked Canadians as much as it shocked Americans. The result was new laws regarding gas tanks, seat belts, safety seats for children, lights and interior design. All of these changes saved thousands of lives but cost the companies millions of dollars to implement.

After the oil shock, American lawmakers also began to regulate the industry's fuel economy and emissions standards. First, the American government sought to reduce some of the pollutants that were unquestionably spewing from millions of cars. In this case, Canadians cars were affected by Californian sensitivities. The state was the first to implement emission standards in an effort to relieve a hazy, choking Los Angeles, the most auto-intensive city in North America. The United States government followed California's lead. Carmakers were required to dramatically reduce the damaging emissions that their engines produced in an effort to fight smog and improve air quality. Further regulations removed lead from gasoline and tightened the rules for the disposal of vehicles, reducing the pollutants they created over the entire life cycle of a car.

At the same time, the government looked to

Before the OPEC embargo: A 1972 Ford Maverick, designated an "Olympic" for the Canadian market, was a classic big American car.

lower Americans' dependency on foreign oil. This meant legislating the auto industry to make smaller, more fuel-efficient cars, a bitter pill to swallow for both American and Canadian car buyers (though perhaps less painful for Canadians). Americans, in particular, loved to buy big cars, known as "gas guzzlers." The American auto industry loved to sell big cars too, since they had the highest profit margins. Fuel-economy regulations became a bête noire of the industry, forcing the Big Three to redesign vehicles by shortening, lightening and narrowing them. The tail fins of the 1950s were a thing of the past, as were the big powerful engines of the period.

Instead of fashion or fad, fuel efficiency and economy became the watchwords of auto design and marketing. By the end of the 1970s, American cars, which had been seen as the central ingredient in a utopian vision of life in North America for much of the post-war period, were now viewed with much less romance. The beautiful, stylish cars

of the golden age gave way to the unattractive, practical autos of an era of austerity.

These steps signalled a sea change in attitudes toward the automobile. In 1970, the first Earth Day was celebrated by more than twenty million Americans and Canadians and marked a new awareness of the fragility of the planet. For many who worried about Mother Earth, it was clear that the car was a leading cause of the planet's ills. The Clean Air Act, the creation of the Environmental Protection Agency (both in 1970) and the Corporate Average Fuel Economy (CAFE) regulations of 1975 were all, to some degree, designed to rein in the unabated rule of the car and its consumptive ways.

The stream of laws from the US Congress resulted in a tidal wave of regulation that was unleashed upon the American auto industry and spilled over into Canada. With the two industries combined into one, the Canadian factories had to maintain standards imposed upon the

The new age: Honda came to Canada in the 1980s. Here, the production of Acura "cross-over utility vehicles" (CUVs) takes place in Alliston, Ontario.

companies by US legislation. When it came to safety and fuel economy, Canadians had no choice but to eventually follow the US lead. These regulations, the oil embargo and a decline in the sale of its vehicles meant that by the mid-1970s the Canadian industry, for the first time since the Depression, faced serious trouble.

The new post–golden age difficulties were epitomized by the woes of the Chrysler Corporation. Chrysler, the smallest of the Big Three, suffered considerably under the onerous new regulatory regime imposed upon it by the government. Brutal competition from the Japanese, bad management and poor cars didn't help either. By 1979, the company, once a shining example of the brilliance and style of Detroit, teetered on the brink of bankruptcy. Chrysler's

Canadian operations, now completely integrated into that of their American parent, were tied down to what was seen as a sinking ship. In Windsor, where Chrysler had its main Canadian operations, the outlook was bleak. In the long winter of 1980, Chrysler left thousands of unsold vehicles to rust on the grounds of the Windsor Raceway. Unemployment in the city was 12 percent, twice the national average.

In the end, the company survived, though just barely. Corporate saviour Lee Iacocca became famous for hawking the company's cars, introducing new products such as the K-car and the minivan (built in Windsor), and preaching cost-cutting and innovative management techniques at the New Chrysler. More importantly, government bailouts, on both sides of the border, provided Chrysler with loan guarantees to keep the company going as they restructured their operations, cutting thousands of blue- and white-collar jobs and closing dozens of plants — though none in Canada. Nonetheless, Chrysler's near death marked the end of the great post-war boom in the auto industry, the beginning of downsizing, and the emergence of a de-industrialized and economically troubled Rust Belt, at least in northeastern America. For many, Chrysler's travails were a microcosm of the broader malaise of the North American economy.

Although Chrysler's problems generated the most headlines, Ford and GM faced their own troubles, as did the rest of the "domestic" industry. A major cause of these problems was the decline of the Big Three in the marketplace. In a decade focused on thriftiness, imports (primarily from Japan) quickly filled the void as American and Canadian consumers snapped up the smaller, more fuel-efficient and less expensive vehicles. By the end of the 1970s, Honda, Toyota, Nissan, Mitsubishi and other Japanese nameplates had carved out a large and growing segment of the market.

In 1981, Canadians purchased more than 200,000 Japanese-built vehicles, nearly one-fifth of the total market. In the United States, as in Canada, a growing outcry over these imports prompted the Japanese manufacturers to agree to voluntary export restraints. This included the dramatic decision by the Canadian government in 1982 to begin an enormously time-consuming and expensive car-by-car inspection of Japanese imports at the Port of Vancouver. This was intended to send the Japanese a message about the huge numbers of imports, which were flooding into the Canadian market at a time when Canadian auto workers were being laid off by the thousands. A federal government report in 1983 sent a further message when it proposed limiting the Canadian market to companies that built locally.

The arrival of the Japanese transformed both the consumption and the production of cars in Canada. Honda's massive facility in southern Ontario under construction, 1985.

The Japanese response to these threats was to build factories in North America. The first of these appeared in the United States in the early 1980s. Although the Japanese multinationals had decided to establish "transplant" manufacturing operations in the United States, it was less clear as to whether they would do so in Canada as well. Eventually, however, the Japanese firms decided to set up branch plants in Canada: Honda was first, in Alliston, Ontario, in 1986; Toyota built its own facilities at Cambridge, Ontario, in 1988; Canadian Auto Manufacturing Industries (CAMI), a joint Suzuki-GM venture, opened its doors in Ingersoll, Ontario, in 1989. These massive Japanese investments, totaling billions of dollars and thousands of jobs, represented a new generation of foreign plants in

Non-Big Three pride: Studebaker remained independent, with its own Canadian plant, until the 1960s. Two prize models on display.

Canada. They also reflected the growing globalization of the auto industry, of which Canada was at the forefront.

Although they signalled a significant step forward in the development of the sector, the Japanese transplants were not the first new entrants into the Canadian car industry in the post-war period. Three examples of manufacturing efforts — all of which eventually failed — reflected the continuing uniqueness of the Canadian auto sector, even within the continental and global challenges it faced after 1945.

The first of these is the story of Studebaker in Canada, which began, and ended, even before the 1973 shock. Studebaker, like Ford, Chrysler, General Motors, Hudson, Packard, Reo and a number of other American firms, had originally set up shop in Canada in the initial boom times of the auto industry, opening a plant in Windsor in 1910. Production had ceased, however, during the Depression in 1936 and had not restarted

during the war. In 1947, Studebaker, drawn to the potential of the suburban baby boom and the prosperity of post-war Canada, re-entered the Canadian market, taking over a munitions factory in Hamilton, Ontario.

For the next twenty years, Studebaker's Hamilton factory would follow the roller-coaster fortunes of its parent firm, located in South Bend, Indiana. In good times and bad (including a merger with the Packard Corporation in 1956), Studebaker in Canada continued to produce a few car models and maintained a small but loyal following. By the early 1960s, the parent company was on its last legs, a victim of the relentless competition in the industry. Determined to keep going (and to avoid numerous lawsuits from its dealers), the company's management decided to suspend production at the Indiana plant and just build cars in Canada.

For the first time since the demise of Gray-Dort Motors in 1925, Canada had its own auto

The last Studebaker ever built: Photographed at the 2007 Canadian International Auto Show in Toronto, this model rolled off the assembly line in 1966.

company. While it was still wholly American owned and produced cars that were designed in the United States largely for the American market, Studebaker Canada was, as its advertisements proclaimed, "Canada's Own Car." Between 1964 and 1966, the Hamilton plant produced 45,000 cars, nearly three-quarters of which were exported to the United States. The plant also had a special deal with the Hamilton police department to build cruisers for the hometown force. Studebaker maintained a popular position in the Canadian market and, for a short time, was a Canadian success story.

But the realities of the modern car market soon caught up to Hamilton's plucky little factory. Without a full line of cars, Studebaker was not an attractive proposition for many car buyers. Worse, although the company had managed to carve out a niche in the market with its smaller, more economic cars. After 1960, GM, Ford and Chrysler all introduced products in this price and size bracket. And while the Hamilton plant showed a small profit, the Indiana corporation, which had branched out into other consumer products after killing off its auto production in the United States, was not inclined to maintain such a minor operation. In 1966, it was announced to the 700 Studebaker Canada employees that production would cease. The last Studebaker rolled off the assembly line in March 1966.

Somewhat more successful was another foreign

Nova Scotia was the site of the first foreign transplant in North America: Volvos being assembled in Halifax, 1963.

venture in Canada, this time from Sweden. In 1963, Volvo opened its first plant outside of Sweden in an abandoned factory in Dartmouth, Nova Scotia. The opening was heralded as Nova Scotia's chance to become an industrial New Sweden and was even attended by Prince Bertil, son of the Swedish monarch. Drawn by the possibility that Canadians would take to the rugged and dependable vehicles (Volvo reasoned that the two countries shared a similar climate) and generous government assistance, Volvo decided to ship partially knocked-down cars to Canada for reassembly and sale as Volvo Canadians.

Like the Studebaker cars, Canadians initially welcomed these vehicles in a nationalistic embrace. Hundreds of Canadians sought out jobs at the plant, and production jumped from 1,000 cars in 1963 to nearly 5,000 in 1968, and more than 10,000 in 1973. But the company

reached a peak in 1975, building 13,000 vehicles, after which production dropped to under 10,000 a year. By the late 1990s, when the plant was still in operation, Volvo's Halifax factory was producing barely 7,000 cars a year. In a world where average factory production was more than 200,000 vehicles, Volvo's Canadian venture was too expensive and impractical to maintain. In 1998, it was announced that the Swedish experiment in Canada would end. Although the plant's 200 unionized workers protested the terms of their severance packages by taking control of the facility, they eventually agreed to its closure. The last Canadian-built Volvo, a C70, rolled off the assembly line in December 1998 and was donated by the company and its workers to a local hospital.

Far more famous than either Studebaker or Volvo's Canadian stories was that of the Bricklin. Malcolm Bricklin, the car's colourful promoter, had earlier gained success in the industry by bringing Japanese Subaru cars to the United States. In the early 1970s, he convinced the New Brunswick government of Richard Hatfield to provide financial support for his unique gull-winged sports car. Betting that the car could vitalize the province's manufacturing sector, Hatfield lent Bricklin the money and helped him establish a plant in Saint John. With great fanfare and publicity, the cars went into production in 1974. But building a brand new car, particularly a flashy high-maintenance sports car immediately after the 1973 oil crisis and during one of the North American auto industry's most difficult periods, did not bode well. Nor did it help that the car quickly became known as something of a lemon. Sales sputtered. By 1976, the company went bankrupt, with less than 3,000 cars built. Bricklin owed the government $23 million. The catastrophe became something of a punchline and provided a cautionary tale of the perils of government intervention.

The Bricklin may have been Canada's most spectacular (and collectable) automotive failure. Only 3,000 were built in New Brunswick before the company went bankrupt in 1976.

Though the company was a failure, the car, however, quickly passed into automotive lore. With its distinct design, quirky name and unintended rarity, Bricklins became sought-after collector's items. In 1996, Canada Post even issued a stamp commemorating the Bricklin, while the Royal Canadian Mint produced a special $20 silver coin with an image of the car in 2003.

These three stories — Studebaker, Volvo and Bricklin — all illustrate the connections between nationalism, continentalism and globalization in the post-war auto industry. While the three companies were all foreign, they were all accepted, at least initially, as Canadian success stories. They also each attempted to take advantage of Canada's continental connection to the United States by producing for that automobile market, the world's largest. They are global stories in that they illustrate the reach of the car industry around the world: Volvo was a Swedish company building in Canada for the United States; Studebaker was an American company in

Canada; and Malcolm Bricklin was himself an American who had been originally successful importing Japanese cars to North America and tried to find fame and fortune by making New Brunswick an industrial titan. Now Bricklin cars are prized around the world.

In the post-embargo auto world, nationalism and continentalism also became increasingly important for Canadian auto labour. Since the 1940s, George Burt's Canadian United Auto Workers (UAW) had sometimes chafed at the demands placed upon Canadian workers by their "International." The UAW's headquarters at Solidarity House in Detroit often dictated policy, even when it went against Canadian workers' interests. By the 1970s, with the tumultuous upheaval in the industry and demands by the Big Three for concessions and job cuts, Canadian workers had had enough. Burt's successor, the fiery Bob White, resented the UAW's control over Canadian affairs, particularly contract negotiations.

Toyota, the world's most successful auto maker in the twenty-first century, built a Canadian plant in Cambridge, Ontario, in the 1980s, and challenged GM for the global sales title.

When auto workers were hit with the harsh realities of deindustrialization in the early 1980s, White was steadfast that the Canadian union would not give up anything to the corporations. But the American UAW leadership was of a different mind. After a bruising fight with Detroit over GM negotiations in 1984 (which led to a strike), White led the Canadian arm of the union out of the International UAW and to independence in 1985. White, and the new Canadian Auto Workers (CAW), realized that because the Auto Pact had integrated the industry continentally, Canadian workers held an advantage. Canadian workers built cars, components and engines for all of the Big Three operations. If they went on strike in Canada, they could paralyze not only the Canadian part of the industry, but most of the whole North American sector as well. The CAW reflected the ongoing vibrancy of nationalism both within the Canadian auto industry and the country at large, even in a world constrained by continentalism and buffeted by global winds.

By the mid-1980s, this nationalism was being sorely tested. The government of Progressive Conservative Prime Minister Brian Mulroney embarked on a plan to implement a comprehensive free trade agreement with the United States. While US President Ronald Reagan himself was a committed free trader (notwithstanding the export restraints on cars he "voluntarily" negotiated with the Japanese), the American Congress was becoming more protectionist. Many Canadians, particularly Ontarians and their government, and the CAW, were fearful that the end of the Auto Pact would mean the end of the Canadian auto industry. Advocates of free trade, such as Mulroney and many business executives, argued that any new agreement would protect the auto industry and lead to even more auto trade between the two countries. When the final deal was consummated in 1989, the two sides established new rules that effectively ended the Auto Pact but protected the Big Three on their home turf in North America.

The free trade agreement coincided with a significant recovery in the North American industry by the mid-1980s. This boom was followed by a dizzying decade of uneven performance for the Detroit-based industry, which lasted well into the twenty-first century. Although the free trade agreement took a continental approach, the Canadian industry itself became increasingly dominated by global developments. Global competition and consolidation in the sector had a direct impact upon the lives of Canadians in places such as Windsor, Oshawa and Oakville. GM, Ford and Chrysler were no longer the only game in town but part of a multinational chess match for dominance. Indeed, in the 1990s, Chrysler was purchased by Daimler-Benz of Germany, Ford bought Britain's Jaguar and Sweden's Volvo, while GM took stakes in Italy's Fiat and Sweden's Saab. All the while, Japanese, Korean and European cars became an everyday part of the automotive landscape in Canada.

During this period, the Canadian industry reached new peaks of success. In 1999, Canada produced three million cars, nearly double the number of vehicles that the country consumed. The vast majority of this production was shipped south to the American market. The Canadian parts sector, which had flourished under the Auto Pact, largely continued its success too, as companies such as Magna, Linamar and Wescast became leading employers in the industry. In fact, the Canadian-owned parts sector became perhaps the most visible success story of the Canadian industry, employing thousands of

The first-generation Honda Civic was not only economical when it came to gas, it actually met emission standards. Millions of Hondas were sold in North America in the 1970s.

Canadians across the country and providing billions of dollars in investment, research and development and head-office benefits.

On the assembly side, in 2005, for the first time in history, Ontario passed Michigan as the leading builder of automobiles in North America. However, the particulars of this unprecedented change in the automotive manufacturing landscape reflected the evolution of the industry since the end of the golden age. While the Big Three still build many cars in Ontario, the Japanese manufacturers in the province constituted a large and growing chunk of production. By the turn of the century, the three Japanese plants in Ontario — Honda, Toyota and CAMI — were producing more than 600,000 vehicles annually. Ontario was the only jurisdiction in the world to be home to six different manufacturers. Canadians, reflecting global trends, heralded these new producers, whose quality cars became, for many, the new benchmark of the sector.

Throughout all these dramatic changes in the industry, Canadians remained loyal to the automobile, if not necessarily to the Big Three. For all

The recovery of the auto industry in the 1980s and 1990s was marked by the success of the SUV, or "sport utility vehicle." These giant vehicles were a testament to the ongoing North American fascination with large cars.

of the challenges it faced after 1973, the car retained its potency as one of society's deepest and most visible influences. From car racing, to highway construction, to the proliferation of different kinds of vehicles (from minivans to SUVs to hybrids), the post-embargo world remained one in which the car still had a prominent place. The pervasive, continuing presence of a roadside automobile culture further illustrated Canadians' attachment to their cars.

But the optimism that had personified attitudes toward cars in the golden age had given way to a more realistic approach toward the automobile. Canadians understood the incredible significance of the automobile industry upon the prosperity of their nation (particularly in Ontario) and their economy as a whole. In the early twenty-first century, the industry generated more than $100 billion in production and employed 150,000 people directly. They also understood that the automobile remained, for all its perceived ills, the first choice of Canadians for their personal transportation and a part of their lives that would remain so for the foreseeable future. In 2005, there were more than eighteen million vehicles registered in Canada. It was difficult to imagine a world without cars, and Canadians' dependence upon the automobile was obvious.

Yet Canadians also began to understand that the car was not consequence-free. It wasn't just the 1970s oil shocks, or the Chrysler near-death experiences, or the extremely cyclical performance of the industry since the 1990s. Their concerns were even more fundamental. There were serious environmental challenges that stemmed from Canadians' continued, and growing, use of automobiles. Questions about the car's sustainability in a fragile world became more and more prominent, as the air, land and water increasingly came to be affected by the car's presence and use. Were the immeasurable benefits bestowed by the automobile — the sense of freedom and self, the ability to work and travel great distances, the standard of living the industry conferred, the very convenience of the machine — outweighed by its costs?

Since its first appearance on Canadian roads more than a century ago, the car had always represented progress, modernity and the ability of technology to make our lives easier. If asked, most Canadians would say that the car has made the world a better place, and continues to do so. They would also recognize that the car, for all its immediate and personal connections and connotations, remains linked to nation, continent and planet in innumerable ways. In the twenty-first century, the car also remains a wellspring of human ingenuity and innovation. New technologies — from the fuel cell, to hybrids, to electrics — hold out the promise of even grander possibilities for the car in the future. Paradoxically, the car may hold the answer to many of the planet's current ills, and much of its future prosperity.

Cars, Canadians and the Twenty-first Century

The car reshapes the city. London, Ontario's downtown in 1960 reflected the central place of the automobile in Canadian life.

At the beginning of the twenty-first century, the car has come to represent much of what we as Canadians see as elemental to our world. The car signifies a level of personal freedom and opportunity unprecedented in human history. As we drive it, it carves its way across our countryside, shapes our cities, our towns, our very landscape to a degree that makes it almost impossible to imagine the world before the car. Our homes are built around the car, as is almost every aspect of our day-to-day lives, from how we consume, to how we work, travel, play, date, and do countless other things that would otherwise be impossible because of the constraints of distance and time.

The automobile also represents economic opportunity. Today, a century after the first Model T came rolling off of the assembly line, the automobile and all of the industries and services it affects provide employment for an astounding one in seven Canadians. It remains the single most important economic activity in Canada, constituting the largest slice of production, exports, imports and employment. The car has transformed us from a nation of hewers of wood and drawers of water to makers of parts

Rush hour: Car-oriented Montreal, and much of Canada and North America, faces the challenges of traffic, pollution and gasoline prices.

and assemblers of cars. Without the car, Canadians would be far less prosperous, both on an individual and a national level. The taxes generated by automobiles and the auto industry constitute an important component of governmental revenues.

As a symbol of Canadians' prosperity and way of life, the car has become one of the country's most important icons. Cars link Canadians in a manner that the railways once did. They allow Canadians to travel their great country, and to make, each day, the connections between people and places that help to define Canada. In doing so, they also illustrate Canadians' place in North America. Canadians' car legacy is as much a unique story as it is one that is solidly grounded in a continental commonality. As a car nation, Canada would not exist if it were not for the pervasive, prevailing influence of the world's greatest automotive country, the United States.

The automobile also connects Canadians to the larger world in countless ways. It is not just the billions of dollars of automotive cars and parts that Canadians export, primarily to the United States, but to dozens of other countries as

well. The globalization of the industry, in which a car that a Canadian drives might have parts from three different continents, is just but one aspect of this global connectedness. More importantly, the car and its industry are intimately connected to the most important geopolitical, environmental and ideological questions of our time.

The global pursuit of oil, which has become the world's most sought-after commodity, is because of the car. Embargoes, wars and strategic diplomacy around the world are a direct consequence of the use of the car, particularly in North America. The global oil game also plays a role in domestic Canadian politics: battles over the consumption and ownership of Alberta's vast oil reserves were a political hot button between Ottawa and the West in the 1970s and 1980s. More recently, the question of oil revenues has come to define federal-provincial relations for provinces such as Newfoundland and Nova Scotia because of their new-found oil wealth.

The battle over oil for cars is also part of a broader environmental reassessment of the automobile that Canadians have been making since the 1960s. The burning of fossil fuels has become an uncontested cause of global warming and one of the greatest concerns for Canadians and people around the world. The exploitation of Alberta's vast oil sands puts Canadians at the forefront of this debate. The international effort to curb greenhouse gas emissions, of which automobiles constitute a significant contribution, has become one of the great movements of our time and a litmus test for many Canadians about what kind of world they want to leave their children and grandchildren. Global awareness over the detrimental impact of the automobile has become a key social, political and economic question, one that crosses borders and affects people from all walks of life. The car is, in many measures, the centrepiece of this global issue.

Toronto's ZENN Motor Company cars being assembled. ZENN (Zero Emission, No Noise) is a leader in fuel-efficient, environmentally safe cars.

Around the world, and in Canada too, governments, car companies, environmental activists and ordinary people are debating, demanding changes and making consumer choices around the question of the car's impact upon the environment.

The car connects Canadians to their world well beyond the air-changing or landscape-shaping impact of the automobile. The September 11, 2001, attacks on the World Trade Center and the Pentagon illustrated the linkages between the automobile and pivotal international events. The most immediate effect was to bring the Canada–United States border to a standstill, causing massive disruption and stopping more than $1 billion in daily automotive trade. At the Windsor–Detroit corridor, the busiest and most important cross-border passage in the world, trucks, cars and people were backed up for days and weeks. In the months after the attacks, the auto industry was involved in another manner: in an effort to maintain consumer confidence in the wake of the attacks, Detroit's Big Three, led by General Motors, cut their car prices. For many observers, this decision was key in avoiding an economic downturn. September 11, 2001, and its aftermath were, to some degree, very much about the car.

The interconnectedness of the car to the great political, environmental and economic questions of our time is a testament to the automobile's continuing centrality in both our daily lives and in the great historical shifts that the car itself ushered in at the dawn of the twentieth century. In a very real way, every time we use the car, it re-establishes a link from our own notions of ourselves and what it means to be "modern" to the distant, hazy past of Henry Ford, Gordon McGregor, Jack Haney and George Burt. The automobiles that shaped those

The past: The original economical car, a 1914 Model T.

peoples' lives and our own cars have remained fundamentally unchanged for more than a century: the vast majority of cars still ride on air-inflated rubber tires, use internal combustion engines and have two or four doors. Each time we use a car, we are reaffirming our connection to the past, continuing to live the imagined futures that Ford and McGregor wanted for the people who bought and used their cars. Cars are, ultimately, living history.

But they are much more than that too. They are an undeniable part of our future. While the car faces many challenges, from environmental problems to geopolitical issues, no one is making the argument that the auto should be banned or that cars do not hold as important a place in transportation in the twenty-first century as they did in the twentieth century. Ultimately, the persistence of the car forces us to ask the question: what will the future of the car hold for Canadians?

Since the time of the Model T, the technology and production processes of the automobile have been seen by many as the epitome of progress. The advances in lifestyle, convenience and opportunity brought by mass automobility were no less important than the economic benefits that the auto industry generated. But these technologies and processes came to be questioned in the second half of the twentieth century. The problems associated with the automobile came to be seen, by many, as outweighing the car's benefits. If the internal combustion engine and the assembly line did not represent the height of technology and work, what were the alternatives?

Our dependence upon technology, particularly the car, exposes both the innovations we are capable of and our shortcomings in using technology in a responsible manner. The car as we know it is not a technological failure, but the cost of millions of cars on the roads does pose a monumental challenge. Slowly but surely we are beginning to address this challenge. And we are doing so largely through technology. Whether it be improving old technologies, such as the internal combustion engine, or reinventing discarded technologies, such as the electric car, or inventing entirely new technologies, such as fuel cells and hybrids, the promise of automotive technology is abundant. While many of these technological advances are being made around the world, Canadians have a hand in making this promise become a reality. From Ballard's fuel cell research in Vancouver, to Toronto's innovative electric ZENN car, to the public/private AUTO21 Research Network, Canadians are building a new future for the car. There is no doubt that in the next fifty or one hundred years cars will still exist largely as they have since the Model T, but there will be differences too. Cars will run cleaner, smarter and safer, and last longer. The question is whether those advances will come in time to save us from the cumulative problems that a century of automobility has wrought.

If you asked most Canadians, they would say that they have no doubt that the car is here to stay, in some form or another. Personal mobility through the automobile is so fundamental to our existence that while we may question its con-

The future? A 2007 model ZENN car.

sequences and work to improve it, few would suggest that we get rid of cars entirely. They might be a little more concerned with the future of auto work: after all, there is no Godgiven right for Canadians to have a vibrant and growing auto industry, and many changes in the Canadian, North American and global auto sector — from trade rules, to health care costs, to the value of the Canadian dollar — both threaten and provide benefits to the Canadian auto industry. Canadians might also be a little ambivalent about their own use of the car, given the environmental challenges and practical realities of auto gridlock on many Canadian roads.

Nonetheless, the future of the car remains a salient question for many Canadians. History teaches us that at the end of the nineteenth century the car came as a revolution and spread so quickly and thoroughly that it utterly remade Canadian society. For more than a century, Canadians have continued to live with this automobile revolution and all the consequences and permutations that it represents. As we begin the twenty-first century, another automobile revolution is unfolding, one which will no doubt challenge, but not likely change, Canada as a car nation.

Related Sites and Museums

Antique Automobile Museum

The museum showcases vintage and antique automobiles and other equipment related to transportation and communication history.

31 Principale Street
Saint-Jacques, NB E7B 1V6
www.tourismnewbrunswick.ca

Assiniboia and District Museum

The museum's theme is the growth of Assiniboia from its first residents in 1913 to modern day. It is one of the most impressive and modern museums in south-central Saskatchewan and has more than twenty vintage vehicles on display.

506 3rd Avenue West
Assiniboia, SK
(306) 642-5353
assini.museum@sasktel.net
www.assiniboia.net/html/visiting/museum.html

Canada Science and Technology Museum

A "hands-on" museum boasting hundreds of vehicles, the Canada Science and Technology Museum helps the public to understand the ongoing relationships between science, technology and Canadian society.

1867 St. Laurent Boulevard
Ottawa, ON K1G 5A3
www.sciencetech.technomuses.ca

Canadian Automotive Museum

The museum's mission is to illustrate and educate Canadians about the role the automotive industry has played in the economic and social development of Canada. Dozens of vehicles are on display, from the earliest Canadian vehicles to the mainstays of the industry in the twentieth century.

99 Simcoe Street South
Oshawa, ON L1G 4G7
(905) 576-1222
www.oshawa.ca/tourism/can_mus.asp

Canadian Motorsports Hall of Fame

Canada's leading collection of racing vehicles and the primary source of historical motorsport information.

8220 Fifth Line
Halton Hills, ON L7G 4S6
www.cmhf.ca

Canadian Museum of Civilization

As the national museum of human history, the Canadian Museum of Civilization is committed to fostering in all Canadians a sense of their common identity and their shared past. Vehicles and automobile-related materials throughout the collection.

100 Laurier Street
Gatineau, QC K1A 0M8
www.civilization.ca/visit/indexe.aspx

Canadian Transportation Museum and Heritage Village (Windsor)

The Canadian Transportation Museum is a state-of-the-art facility. It houses various modes of transportation, from the mid-1800s up to the 1992 Dodge Viper. The museum includes horse- and oxen-drawn carts, a 1904 Mitchell horse-drawn hearse, fire trucks, Ford Model Ts and As, hot rods, Corvettes, T-Birds and more.

6155 Arner Townline
County Road 23, RR#2
Kingsville, ON N9Y 2E5
www.ctmhv.com/index.htm

Canadian War Museum

This national museum presents Canada's military past and how it shaped the country. Its outstanding exhibitions explain Canada's rich military history from earliest times to the present, featuring the experiences of people on the battlefields and at home. Hundreds of military vehicles on display.

1 Vimy Place
Ottawa, ON K1A 0M8
www.warmuseum.ca/cwm/cwme.asp

Car Life Museum

The museum presents the history of the vehicle from farm machinery to automobiles. Includes a Cadillac owned by Elvis Presley.

Trans-Canada Highway
between Borden-Carlton and Charlottetown
Bonshaw, PEI
(902) 675-3555

Gilles Villeneuve Museum

Dedicated to the memory of the famous Quebec Formula 1 driver, the museum holds a number of vehicles and memorabilia related to Villeneuve and Canadian racing.

960 avenue Gilles-Villeneuve
Berthierville, QC J0K 1A0
(Highway 40, Exit 144)
www.museegillesvilleneuve.com

Manitoba Antique Auto Museum

The museum is home to one of the most extensive antique automobile collections in North America, including early Fords, Hupmobiles, Overlands and Russell-Knights.

Box 477
Elkhorne, MB
mbautomuseum.com

Museé Antique Victor Bélanger

Located in a historical village in a natural landscape that includes a schoolhouse, a chapel, a general store, a saloon and a sugarhouse, the antique cars museum contains thirty-two antique cars and trucks.

1080, route Kennedy
Saint-Côme-Linière, Beauce, QC G0M 1J0
www.museevbelanger.com

New Brunswick Museum

Opened in 1996, New Brunswick's largest museum contains exhibits on the natural and human history of the province. Vehicles include a Bricklin car.

Market Square
Saint John, NB E2L 4Z6
www.nbm-mnb.ca

Nixdorf Classic Car Museum

The museum houses nearly one hundred vintage cars lovingly restored to their original condition mostly from the 1930s to 1960s, including a 1947 Plymouth Roadster and a 1955 Ford Thunderbird.

15809 Logie Road
Summerland, BC V0H 1Z6
(250) 494-4111
www.nixdorfclassiccars.com

Parkwood National Historic Site

Once home to auto baron R. Samuel McLaughlin (founder of General Motors of Canada), Parkwood is a rare surviving example of the type of wealthy estate developed in Canada during the inter-war years.

270 Simcoe Street North
Oshawa, ON L1G 4T5
www.parkwoodestate.com

Reynolds-Alberta Museum

An Alberta-oriented museum specializing in the preservation and exhibition of transportation, aviation, agriculture and industry exhibits. Artifacts include a 1929 Duesenburg Phaeton Royale Model J and a 1913 Chevrolet Classic Six, the oldest known production Chevrolet in the world.

Box 6360
Wetaskiwin, AB T9A 2G1
www.machinemuseum.net

Victoria Auto Racing Hall of Fame

An institution dedicated to preserving the memory and future of racing in BC and in Canada. Dozens of rare and unique race cars on display.

7908 Pelter Place
Saanichton, BC V8M 1K6
www.victoriaautoracinghalloffame.com

Further Reading

Anastakis, Dimitry. *Auto Pact: Creating a Borderless North American Auto Industry, 1960–1971*. Toronto: University of Toronto Press, 2005.

—. "Between Nationalism and Continentalism: State Auto Industry Policy and The Canadian UAW, 1960–1970." *Labour/Le Travail*, 53 (Spring 2004):87–124.

—. "From Independence to Integration: The Corporate Evolution of the Ford Motor Company of Canada, 1904–2004." *Business History Review*, 78 (Summer 2004):213–53.

—. "Building a 'New Nova Scotia': State Intervention, the Auto Industry, and the Case of Volvo in Halifax, 1963–1996." *Acadiensis*, 34 (Autumn, 2004):3–30.

Ankli, Robert E., and Fred Frederiksen. "The Influence of American Manufacturers on the Canadian Automobile Industry." *Business and Economic History*, Vol. 9, 1981:101–103.

Asher, Robert, and Ronald Edsforth, eds. *Autowork*. Albany: State University of New York Press, 1995.

Beigie, Carl. *The Canada–U.S. Automotive Agreement*. Montreal: The Canadian-American Committee, 1970.

Bladen, Vincent. *Royal Commission on the Automotive Industry*. Ottawa: Queen's Printer, 1961.

Bloomfield, Gerald T. "No Parking Here to Corner: London Reshaped by the Automobile, 1911–61." *Urban History Review*, 1989 18(2):139–58.

Critchlow, Donald T. *Studebaker: The Life and Death of an American Corporation*. Bloomington: Indiana University Press, 1996.

Davies, Stephen. "'Reckless Walking Must be Discouraged': The Automobile Revolution and the Shaping of Modern Urban Canada to 1930." *Urban History Review*, 1989 18(2):123–138.

Davis, Donald F. "Dependent Motorization: Canada and the Automobile in the 1930s." *Journal of Canadian Studies*, 1986 21(3):106–32.

Dummitt, Christopher. "A Crash Course in Manhood: Men, Cars and Risk in Postwar Vancouver." Dimitry Anastakis, ed. *The Sixties: Passion, Politics and Style*. Montreal and Kingston: Queen's University Press, 2008:71–98

Dykes, James G. *Canada's Automotive Industry*. Toronto: McGraw-Hill Co. of Canada, 1970.

Flink, James. *The Automobile Age*. Harvard University Press: Cambridge, MA, 1990.

Gindin, Sam. *The Canadian Auto Workers: The Birth and Transformation of a Union*. Toronto: James Lorimer & Co., 1995.

Halberstram, David. *The Reckoning*. New York: Morrow, 1986.

Harris, Richard. *Creeping Conformity, How Canada Became Suburban, 1900–1960*. Toronto: University of Toronto Press, 2004.

Holmes, John. *The Break Up of an International Labour Union: Uneven Development in the North American Auto Industry and the Schism in the UAW*. Montreal and Kingston: McGill-Queen's University Press, 1990.

Hood, Hugh. *The Motor Boys in Ottawa: A Novel*. Toronto: Stoddart, 1986.

Hyde, Charles K. *Riding the Roller Coaster: A History of the Chrysler Corporation*. Detroit: Wayne State University Press, 2003.

Keeley, James F. "Cast in Concrete for All Time? The Negotiation of the Auto Pact." *The Canadian Journal of Political Science*, Vol. XVI, no. 2 (June 1983):281–98.

Kirton, John. "The Politics of Bilateral Management: The Case of the Automotive Trade." *International Journal*, Vol. 36, 1980–1981:39–69.

Mays, James. *Ford and Canada: 100 Years Together*. Montreal: Syam Publishing, 2003.

Maxcy, George. *The Multinational Automobile Industry*. New York: St. Martin's Press, 1981.

McCarthy, Tom. *Auto Mania: Cars, Consumers and the Environment*. New Haven: Yale University Press, 2007.

Milkman, Ruth. *Farewell to the Factory: Auto Workers in the late Twentieth Century.* Berkeley: University of California Press, 1997.

Molot, Maureen Appel, ed. *Driving Continentally: National Policies and the North American Auto Industry.* Ottawa: Carleton University Press, 1993.

Norton, Peter. "Street Rivals: Jaywalking and the Invention of the Motor Age Street." *Technology and History* 2007 48 (2): 331–59.

Penfold, Steve. " 'Are We to Go Literally to the Hot Dogs?' Parking Lots, Drive-ins, and the Critique of Progress in Toronto's Suburbs, 1965–1975." *Urban History Review*, 2004 33(1): 8–23.

Perry, Ross. *The Future of Canada's Auto Industry: The Big Three and the Japanese Challenge.* Toronto: James Lorimer & Co., 1982.

Rae, John B. *The American Automobile Industry.* Boston: Twayne Publishers, 1984.

Roberts, David. *In the Shadow of Detroit: Gordon M. McGregor, Ford of Canada, and Motoropolis.* Detroit: Wayne State University Press, 2006.

Robertson, Heather. *Driving Force: The McLaughlin Family and the Age of the Car.* Toronto: McClelland and Stewart, 1995.

Sugiman, Pamela H. *Labour's Dilemma: the Gender Politics of Auto Workers in Canada, 1937–1979.* Toronto: University of Toronto Press, 1994.

Thomas, Kenneth P. *Capital Beyond Borders: States and Firms in the Auto Industry, 1960–1994.* New York: St. Martin's Press, 1996.

Traves, Tom. "The Development of the Ontario Automobile Industry to 1939." Ian Drummond, ed. *Progress Without Planning: The Economic History of Ontario from Confederation to the Second World War.* Toronto: University of Toronto Press, 1987.

United Automobile Workers, Canadian Region. *The UAW in Canada.* Windsor, Ontario: UAW Publishing, 1960.

Weintraub, Sidney, and Christopher Sands, eds. *The North American Auto Industry Under NAFTA.* Washington, D.C.: The CSIS Press, 1998.

Wells, Don. "The Impact of the Postwar Compromise on Canadian Unionism: The Formation of an Auto Worker Local in the 1950s." *Labour/Le Travail*, Vol. 36, Fall, 1995:147–73.

White, Richard. *Making Cars in Canada: A Brief History of the Canadian Automobile Industry.* Ottawa: Canada Science and Technology Museum, 2007.

Wilkins, Mira, and Frank Ernest Hill. *American Business Abroad: Ford on Six Continents.* Detroit: Wayne State University Press, 1964.

Yates, Charlotte. *From Plant to Politics: The Autoworkers Union in Postwar Canada.* Philadelphia: Temple University Press, 1993.

Acknowledgements   Visual Credits

When Lynn Schellenberg, my editor at Lorimer, approached me to write a short history of the automobile in Canada, I was not sure it could be done, given the complexity and scope of the story. But her belief in the project and her hard work has made this book possible. My first note of appreciation goes to Lynn, copy editor Heather Sangster, proofreader Pamela Martin and everyone else at Lorimer who have done such an excellent job.

Among the many people who made this book possible, I would particularly like to acknowledge Dr. Peter Frise and everyone at AUTO21, a Network of Centres of Excellence devoted to improving automobility in Canada. Peter has recognized that Canadians cannot understand how to build the car of the future without also understanding the automobile's past in this country. I am very grateful for the support that I have received from AUTO21 over the years.

I would also like to thank Meaghan Beaton, my excellent research assistant (and an emerging scholar in her own right) and my students in "The Car in History" course at Trent University for their helpful remarks. Various individuals and institutions have also helped out by providing images and other materials, and I appreciate their efforts. I would particularly like to thank Joe Sarnovsky at Canadian Auto Workers Local 222, John Bowen at the Ford Archives in Dearborn, MI, Garth Wilson at the Canada Science and Technology Museum, Mr. Bill Burt of Windsor, Margaret Houghton at the Hamilton Public Library, Laura Heasman at Honda Canada, Barry Leppan and Paul Cronkwright of the Hamilton Studebaker Drivers Club and Sue Morrow at the Canadian Press.

My greatest debt is to my wife, Victoria, without whom this book could not have been completed. Given that it was written in the first few months after the birth of our son, Jack, Victoria's patience, support and willingness to read my early drafts during such a whirlwind period in our lives was simply wonderful. Though Victoria made the book possible, it is dedicated to Jack, who has brought such joy to both our lives.

Index